Rio, 15.XI.76

To John [illegible]
[illegible] [illegible] to
a closer [illegible]
an feeling a sense
of [illegible] [illegible]
[illegible] [illegible]
[illegible] [illegible]
[illegible] [illegible]
[illegible]
[illegible]
[illegible]

BEYOND POPULISM

BEYOND POPULISM

By

Candido Mendes
President, Candido Mendes University
Rio de Janeiro

Translated by

L. Gray Cowan
Dean, Graduate School of Public Affairs
State University of New York at Albany

Graduate School of Public Affairs
State University of New York at Albany
Albany · 1977

Published by Graduate School of Public Affairs,
State University of New York at Albany,
Albany, New York 12222
Distributed by State University of New York Press
99 Washington Avenue, Albany, New York 12246

Library of Congress Cataloging in Publication Data

Almeida, Candido Antonio Mendes de, 1928–
Beyond populism.

First published in 1974 under title:
Depues del populismo,
impuguacion social y desarrollo
en Americana Latina.
1. Brazil—Politics and government—1954–
2. Latin America—Politics and government—1948–
3. Populism—Latin America—History.
I. Title.
JL2415 1945.A6613   320.9'81'06   76-40257
ISBN 0-87395-803-9

Contents

Translator's Note

This volume is a somewhat adapted version of the original French manuscript written in 1972. The introduction comes from the edition published by Editions CUF (Paris, 1976). A Spanish version of the original text appeared in 1974 as *Despues del populismo, impuguacion social y desarrollo en America Latina,* (Mexico City: Fondo de Cultura Economica, 1974).

The author, Candido Mendes de Almeida, is President of Candido Mendes University in Rio de Janeiro. A prominent Catholic layman in his country and a well-known political scientist, he has written widely on Latin American political and social development.

Perhaps no better understanding of the author's reasons for writing the book can be given than to quote the introduction of the French editor.

> We present this book as a living document of political life in Latin America during the past few years. It constitutes the evolution of thought of a scholar of politics who has been, at the same time, actively engaged in the daily political life of his country. It is the fruit of an intellectual process that constantly questions the actions of the past and the experience of today in an attempt to find the common strands of political phenomena. Even more, it is the reflective self-criticism of an intellectual caught in the web of contemporary history.

I wish to express my deep appreciation to Dr. Carlos Astiz for having first interested me in making this translation and for his helpful advice along the way. My thanks are due also to Mrs. Mary Warburton for her unfailing patience in the preparation of the manuscript at various stages.

L. Gray Cowan
Dean
Graduate School of Public Affairs
State University of New York at Albany

April 1977

Introduction

This is a study of the different forms confrontation takes in society, from simple pressure to the systematic use of violence. We are particularly interested in the authoritarian or technocratic military regimes of Latin America which succeeded populism in the midsixties. Of these the present Brazilian regime is a typical case which offers ground for comparison with Argentinian regimes which followed the fall of President Illia in 1965 and more particularly the presidencies of Onganía and Levingston.

Our thesis is that the present political situation in Latin America is not simply a continuation of the chronic coups d'etat and unconstitutional regimes which have been a constant of Latin American history. Such phenomena doubtless had a necessary function in the semicolonial systems, the coup d'etat being an attempt by the army to reestablish the political equilibrium upset by the oligarchy. However the military movement of 1964 in Brazil appears to depart completely from this older model and a more similar phenomenon may be observed in other key countries of the continent.

This new type of authoritarianism presents one original trait: it does not appear during a phase of economic stagnation, as in the semicolonial period, but at a moment of dynamic social change. In the Argentinian and Brazilian regimes one is struck by the important role the armed forces play and one is tempted to relate it to the apparent explosion of systems of spontaneous development in Latin America. It is even more significant that this new type of regime appears in those countries of Latin America which are socially the most advanced. It might be hypothesized that this type of regime corresponds to the final stage of the development process—industrialization, urbanization, and the formation of internal markets—which affects all Latin American countries. In this sense the technocratic military regimes of Brazil and Argentina embody a model which may yet inspire the less advanced nations that have still not yet reached the phase of spontaneous development that marked the Brazilian situation from 1946–63 and the Argentinian situation from Peronism through Frondizi. The Brazilian case is probably the more pertinent, not because of its general applicability, but because it so clearly represents a particular stage of social and economic evolution. It is therefore on the basis of Brazilian history since 1945 that we will pose questions concerning the evolution of political and economic subsystems in the countries of Latin America and the appearance of confrontation in the entire social process.

Our reflections on these contemporary phenomena can be neither exhaustive nor definitive. The present work is an essay rather than an in-depth analysis based on comprehensive data. It attempts to capture a definite time period in which one type of development strategy was replaced by another. For "spontaneous development" was substituted "a rational speedup of development." It will have attained its objective if it opens up new perspectives in the interpretation of a less known period of recent Latin American history.

1 Historical overview

Essential characteristics

Three principal elements mark postwar Brazilian political life. First, there appears a persistent polarization of the political actors between populists and antipopulists, the followers of Vargas and those opposed to him. The long prewar rule of Getulio Vargas, president from 1930 to 1937, then chief of the "New State" from 1937 to 1945, profoundly influenced the political scene. The events of the past thirty years may, in fact, be analyzed as different stages in the confrontation between his heirs and his detractors. From this point of view, the "revolution" of 1964 can be interpreted as the final victory of the anti-Vargas forces after twenty years of partial domination by the populist alliance.

The second recurring element is that inflation and the growing external debt have destroyed any effort to carry out a coherent long-term policy from one government to another. Efforts at stabilizing inflation based on an orthodox policy of austerity have met strong social resistance and at the very first signs of recession they have given way to policies meant to increase development. These have relaxed credit controls, pressure on wages, and measures to slow down public spending. The external debt, which has increased constantly because of the great need for external assistance, has also exacerbated the "national question" among the more or less convinced partisans of nationalism.

The third characteristic is a carryover from previous decades—the active presence of an armed force ready to intervene when "legal" procedures are blocked or appear "threatened." Virtually no presidential succession was accomplished "constitutionally" during this period and the Brazilian constitutional framework is extremely fragile. Remodeled or changed in 1933, 1937, 1945, 1961, and 1963, the Constitution was suspended in 1964 and replaced by the "Institutional Acts." It was again rewritten in 1967, modified by new Institutional Acts in 1968, and remade again in 1969.

Behind these constants of political life are to be found certain profound givens of Brazilian postwar society. As it has grown out of the neocolonial situation which derived from its newly independent status, Brazil experienced the difficulties of an urbanizing and industrializing society, and these changes were reflected in the play of politics.

Very schematically, the arrival of Getulio Vargas in power in 1930 marked the end of the old Republic. Political life had been carried on by a small elite in a highly decentralized fashion at the state level; the large landowners and large export firms exerted primary political influence. Political life now began to open up to new social classes. The electorate, though it excluded illiterates, took in a growing number of employees and laborers in the cities. Vargas's prewar policy, which was interventionist in the economic field (it supported private enterprise and public investment) and on the social front (the labor code), clearly acknowledged these social changes. The new political orientation can be seen in the strong push toward democracy in postwar Brazil. Populism relied on the alliance of two parties: the Social Democratic Party, which encompassed those traditional social classes who were no longer threatened by social transformation, and the Brazilian Workers' Party, which sought to represent the new forces of urban labor. In the opposite camp, the National Democratic Union regrouped the capitalist enemies of populism and recruited into its ranks numerous conservative groups who were the inheritors of the Old Republic.

In the postwar period there was added to this rivalry a new dimension, deriving from rapid social change, which was expressed in terms of diverging development plans or paraideology (cf. here note 23, ch. III). The relatively optimistic postwar developmental theories in the West put considerable confidence in the intrinsic capacity of social structures to adapt and convert, and they maintained the necessity of stimulating the process of change by government intervention. This concept was defended in Brazil by a group of young economists and lawyers in the Higher Institute of Brazilian Studies, among whom were Helio Jaguaribe, Roberto Campos, and Guerreiro Ramos. Opposed to this theory were the classic conceptions which more scrupulously respected the rules of economic liberalism. Adherents included the economists of the International Monetary Fund. The new social and political forces were divided between these two concepts. The populist alliance, which rested on a more broadly based electorate, favored the developmentalist model, while the conservative inheritors of the Old Republic preferred the neoliberal theories, as did the new Brazilian business elite.

A precarious institutional framework protected by the armed forces, economic fragility, the "national" question, and those who favored or opposed Vargas—these were the constants of postwar Brazilian political life. They arose from the profound change that the development crisis had brought about in society. It was against this background that the chronology of political events unfolded.

Political chronology 1945–70

The pluralist republic, 1945–64 [1]

Because the allied powers won in World War II, Vargas saw that it would be necessary to democratize the regime in Brazil. Presidential and legislative elections were fixed for 2 December 1945 and the political forces began to organize. Within the "insiders," that is to say, those who were within the orbit of Vargas, two parties were created, the PSD (Partido Social Democrático) and the PCB (Partido Communista Brasileiro), to support the campaign of the Vargas candidate, General Dutra. Of the "outsiders" opposed to the populist group, the UDN (União Democrática Nacional), strongly supported by the press, chose another military figure, Brigadier Eduardo Gomes. Although the PCB has been disposed toward a common front with the populists, it ultimately presented its own candidate, a noncommunist. Vargas was the unknown element in the campaign. An initiative on his part was warmly awaited by the "queremists" (a name given to Vargas adherents) but feared by the other political actors. These fears increased when Vargas decided unilaterally to set state and municipal elections for the same day as the federal elections—a decision which entailed the resignation of all those holding political office. Nomination of his brother as head of police in Rio de Janeiro confirmed suspicions that he was planning to rig the elections. After a fruitless attempt at conciliation on the part of General Dutra, the armed forces demanded that Vargas step down on 30 October 1945.

The elections, which took place during the interregnum, in which the chief executive was the president of the Federal Supreme Court, gave an absolute majority to General Dutra. Within the Legislature, the PSD triumphed over the UDN, followed by the PTB (Partido Trabalhista Brasileiro), and lastly the PCB. The order of strength among the three principal parties was to remain the same during the entire period of "pluralism."

The election of General Dutra was a victory for the populist alliance, but his presidency was not specifically populist. Marked by the beginning of the Cold War, its political and economic management conformed to the West's preferences. The communist party was dissolved, and economic policy was inspired by neoliberal principles. True to laissez faire until 1947, the government adopted an orthodox policy of austerity as monetary and financial difficulties grew greater. The period was marked, moreover, by a process of "spontaneous industrialization," [2] which was clearly linked to an overvaluation of the cruzeiro.

Conducted under the new democratic constitution of September 1946, the elections of 30 October 1950 again brought victory to the populist alliance, which was reinforced by the Progressive Socialist Party, the neopopulist party of the São Pauliste, Ademar de Barros. Vargas was elected by a 20 percent majority over his UDN opponent.

Resolved not to rekindle old suspicions or irritate sensitivities, Vargas opted first for a systematic policy of conciliation of the highly socially heterogeneous political forces based on the PSD-PTB and PSP alliance. He even made an overture toward his opponents in the UDN. He followed a moderate economic and international policy, aimed at proving the seriousness of his intentions. In an agreement with the Brazilian United States Commission, he drew up a classical policy for improving the monetary and financial situation.

His strategy was hampered, however, by economic difficulties and growing Cold War tensions. Brazilian political forces polarized as the UDN hardened its rightist position and the army reinforced its anticommunist tendency (May, 1952). Relations with the United States, so necessary to economic recovery, were strained because the new members of the Eisenhower cabinet, Dulles and Humphrey, showed such little interest in Brazilian problems. Vargas then turned to the populist forces and in particular to the trade unions and the

PTB. He increased wages and again took up the theme of nationalism. Petrobas (the nationalized petroleum industry) was created, Electrobras (a nationalized electric power industry) was proposed, and Vargas threatened to apply the law on repatriating profits effectively. The minister of labor, João Goulart, was associated with this more radical political stance.

The economic impasse resulting from the total abandonment of all antiinflation measures and the reaction of liberal conservatives and the army to the radicalization of government led finally to a crisis. Carlos Lacerda, a political journalist, waged a violent campaign in which he accused Vargas of having negotiated an anti-American alliance with Chile and Argentina. An unsuccessful attempt on Lacerda's life prompted inquiries which revealed certain facts of corruption that brought tension to its height. In the armed forces there was a high state of anxiety and impatience. In the face of a demand to resign on 24 August 1954, Vargas committed suicide in the Presidential Palace of Catete.

Vice-President Café Filho, a member of the PST who was on good terms with the UDN, assumed power until the presidential elections scheduled for October 1956. On the political front, the new president sought a policy that conformed to the requirements of American creditors, but after the fall of the neoliberal minister, Eugenio Gudin, Jose Maria Whitaker undertook a new policy of economic expansion.

The presidential campaign of 1956 was marked by the relative cohesion of the populist alliance behind its candidate, Juscelino Kubitscheck (PSD) and uncertainty and defeatism in the adversary's camp. The legislative elections of 1954 had shown the persistent vitality of populism, and the UDN presidential candidate, General Tavora, had little chance of gaining a majority. Certain anti-Vargaists, like Lacerda and some army officers, began to doubt that there was any legal method of coming to terms with populism, and the extreme right opposition presented its own candidate, Plinio Salgado. The elections gave a narrow victory to Juscelino Kubitscheck and João Goulart was elected by a wide majority to the vice-presidency. The antipopulist opposition contested the elections, but after a month of maneuvering some legalistically minded army men, led by General Lott, imposed a decision in favor of the two elected leaders (November 11–12, 1956).

Under the presidency of Juscelino Kubitscheck, the economy experienced a brief period of rapid expansion with an annual increase of 4 percent in per capita production. Overall industrial production increased 80 percent, but the electrical industry and communication rose 380 percent and the transport equipment sector rose 600 percent.

The positive trade balance of this period resulted from Kubitscheck's first years as president, during which time he developed a certain mystique of development while simultaneously improvising an astute policy of alliances and conciliation of interests. Relying on the work of the BrazilianUnited States Commission, the Economic Commission for Latin America, and on the thinking of the young intellectuals of the Institute for Social Research, he defined a "Program of Objectives" conforming to the principles he had set forth during the campaign in his "national development plan." Within the process of import substitution already in operation, industrialization of the basic sectors and the development of infrastructure was to be favored through some degree of state intervention. Clearly anticommunist, Kubitscheck did not foresee a rigid nationalistic statism; the private sector was to be aided in the same way as the public sector, and the frontiers were largely open to foreign capital in association with national enterprises. Kubitscheck sought, moreover, the blessing of the United States and proposed a program of cooperation which was later used as a model for the Alliance for Progress.

Kubitscheck was able to count on a wide base of support for his development program so long as he did not question fundamental social structures. The traditionalists, certain new industrialists and businessmen of São Paulo, as well as young intellectuals and urban workers, were ready to join together around such symbols as the projected new capital. By temperament Kubitscheck was a conciliator. He preferred to defuse tension and conflict by compromise, and rather than reorganize state administrative structures, he preferred to create *ad hoc* organisms such as SUDENE and NOVACAP.

Compromise and improvisation were not sufficient, however, to deal with Brazil's chronic financial and monetary difficulties. After an attempt to return to a policy of stabilization (October 1958) to satisfy the requirements of the SMI, Kubitscheck finally broke off the dialogue with foreign creditors (January 1959). Once again political life

6

began to polarize. Already in the elections of 1958 the PTB had gained a number of seats, and a more radical tendency, led by Leonel Brizola, governor of Rio Grande do Sul and brother-in-law of Goulart, began to appear within the populist alliance. In the campaigns in the Northeast, Francisco Julião encouraged the rural masses to mobilize in peasant leagues, while militants of Action Populaire urged workers to join trade unions.

This beginning of popular mobilization aroused the anxiety of the landowners, the urban middle classes, and the military. As a result, Janio Quadros, governor of the State of São Paulo, was elected president in the elections of October 1960.

An "independent" candidate, supported by the UDN and the Democratic Christian Party, Quadros carried out an ambiguous campaign, which emphasized the necessity of fighting administrative inefficiency and waste. Claiming to favor liberalism and developmentalism simultaneously, Quadros left the details of his policies vague. The six months of his presidency disconcerted both his populist enemies and his UDN allies. After first attempting an orthodox policy, designed to create the monetary and administrative order that would secure him additional American aid, he turned for advice to the developmentalists at the first signs of recession. His allies on the right had little confidence in the stability of his economic policies and they deplored his tendency in foreign policy toward favoring the Third World (he renewed relations with the Soviet Union, had a favorable attitude toward Communist China and a leaning toward Nasser, and he had given a medal to Che Guevarra). On the 25 August 1961 he proposed his resignation to Congress and it was accepted with unseemly haste.

Presidential authority thus came to Vice-President João Goulart, the political figure most feared by the antipopulists. A spiritual son of Getulio Vargas, he had been identified with the most radical wing of the Vargas alliance since the time of his close alliance with the PEB and he had been associated with the trade unions since his period as minister of labor. He was in Communist China at the time of the Quadros resignation and owed his nomination to the extreme division within the military leadership. By an ingenious action Congress resolved the crisis; on 2 September it voted an additional Act to the Constitution, which instituted a semipresidential regime. On 5 September Goulart became president, assisted by a Council of Ministers responsible to the Assembly.

The Goulart government went through three phases. From September 1961 to January 1963 Goulart sought to reestablish the presidential regime, meanwhile making attempts to disarm the anxieties of the conservatives. His foreign policy was one of détente with the United States. Internally he temporized, seeking some equilibrium of forces that would support him. Successive ministerial crises and popular agitation resulting from paralysis of government finally created an atmosphere favorable to reestablishment of the presidential regime, and it was ratified by plebiscite on 6 January 1964.

From January 1963 to June 1964, Goulart relied upon the so-called "positive left" and appointed as ministers Celso Furtado and San Tiago Dantas. In its role as the reformist movement of the left, the "positive left" believed that the contradictory problems of the Brazilian economy could be resolved within the framework of the existing political structure. By means of a triennial plan, they proposed to carry out an antiinflationist policy which would be integrated with a more general policy of development. However, the antiinflationist program became difficult to apply in the face of such a weak overall social consensus. Under strong pressure from a variety of socioeconomic groups, the government was forced to concede higher salary levels, such as the 70 percent raise accorded civil servants and the military, which ruined Brazil's entire credibility with the experts of the international monetary fund.

From June 1963 on, with the departure of Furtado and Dantas, Goulart's policy became more radical and, concomitantly, political forces became more and more polarized. Goulart resolutely followed the orientation of his brother-in-law, Leonel Brizola, who spoke for the "negative left." He sought the support of the trade unions (the General Strike Command and the General Workers' Committee), students (the National Students Union—UNE), the militants of Acão Popular, and the peasant leagues of Francisco Julião. He accentuated the "basic reform" theme first evoked in 1952, which emphasized particularly the question of foreign property and capital in Brazil and agrarian reform. At the same time the right was becoming more organized and more rigid. Within the UDN the Lacerdo faction

8

gained prominence over the more moderate group of Magalhães Pinto. Businessmen and industrialists were united in a patriotic front stemming from the theories of the Institute for Social Research and Study. The army, too, suffered from the current social tension: on 12 September 1963 hundreds of air force and navy subalterns, in cooperation with certain trade union elements, sought to take power in Brasilia. The military conspiracy which finally overthrew the regime began to organize in October 1963.

From October to April the crisis intensified. On the advice of the military ministers, who became more anxious as strikes and new political movements multiplied, Goulart sought to proclaim a government of national emergency. He asked the Congress to vote a state of siege on 4 October 1963, then withdrew his demand three days later when violence exploded killing six people at a protest in a Minas Gerais steel mill. A continuing strike of bank employees increased insecurity. After this stillborn attempt at authoritarian government, Goulart turned resolutely toward the more radical elements and became their leader. On 13 March 1964, at a large mass meeting in the center of Rio set up with the help of the trade unions and the military, Goulart announced two decrees—one nationalizing those petroleum refineries still in private hands and the other making it possible to expropriate land along the internal communication routes and in certain irrigation zones. He announced, moreover, a future revision of foreign mining concessions and the effective application of the law on the repatriation of profits. The projects announced in the decrees were revised and developed two days later in a message to Congress. The right replied by mobilizing protests disguised as religious processions in São Paulo. On 20 March the military intervened, led by the commanding general of the army, Castelo Branco. By 29 March the minister of the navy had been deposed for having imprisoned a trade-union sailor. On 30 March the army mobilized in Minas Gerais and Carlos Lacerda, governor of Rio de Janeiro, arrested the trade union leaders. The general strike set for 30 March failed. Goulart fled to Brasilia, then to Porto Alegre, and Congress finally declared the presidency vacant on 1 April. An Institutional Act created a supreme military command and Castelo Branco was elected president for a period, initially, of three months.

The technocratic military regime, 1964 [3]

Having come to power in the traditional manner in order to establish a legal order, the military remained in power and created a new institutional framework. A year after his investiture, President Costa e Silva was still promising to return to pluralist democracy before the end of his term of office. In fact, however, the ten years from 1964 to 1974 were marked by a consolidation of the regime and a constantly hardening line.

Branco was a representative of the moderate tendency. During his presidency he concentrated on the specific task of restoring economic and administrative order, and he sought to leave the country, on his departure, with a more stable institutional structure.

Elected on 11 April 1964 for three months, he was confirmed in office until 1966 by virtue of Institutional Act I), then until 1967, since it appeared that stabilization required additional delay. Economic recovery was entrusted to Roberto Campos and Roberto Gouveia de Bulhões, who put together a classic stabilization plan—control of monetary resources, reduction in public expense, simplification and rationalization of administration, and control of credit. The plan, although classic, had progressive elements which were designed to reduce the risks of a recession. Despite these precautions, signs of serious slowing down appeared and forced a temporary relaxation of these measures. Relative improvement in the economy was attained by 1967, at the price, however, of a substantial lowering of national production.

On the political front, Castelo Branco's effort to contain the hardliners, who favored a reinforcement of authoritarianism and the maintenance of the military in power, was partially interrupted by the gubernatorial elections of 1965, where the persistent vitality of the populist alliance was clearly shown. In exchange for the confirmation in office of the populist governments of Minas and the State of Guanabara, the executive gained two new Institutional Acts from Congress. By the first of these, political parties were suppressed and replaced by two official groups, the Alliance for National Renewal (ARENA), which supported the government, and the Democratic Movement of Brazil (MDB), which played the role of the opposition. The second Act made the election of the president indirect and fixed it for 1966 (it was later to be put off for a year). This Act also greatly increased presidential power in the guarantee of political liberties (such as removal from office and suspension of political rights). Branco continued to consolidate the institutional framework before his departure and caused a constitution to be voted in 1967 which integrated the essential portions of the decrees and Institutional Acts promulgated since 1964.

Costa e Silva's three-year presidency constituted a great turning point of the regime. Under the benevolent tutelage of Castelo Branco, the new elite had coexisted with the forces of the Old Republic. Most political activists had been integrated into one or another of the new parties. With the improvement in the economic situation, however, demands for liberalization of the regime grew more strident and led to a confrontation.

After 1966 Carlos Lacerda had drifted away from the new leadership. He finally joined with some of his former colleagues and some of his old enemies in a project conceived with the intention of pulling the artificial ARENA into support of moderate and progressive governmental action (the "Frente Ampla"). Others to be found in the new front included Kubitscheck, Quadros, and, in exile, Goulart. This attempted collaboration among the civilian politicians soon brought about a complete polarization of the political scene. The affair began with generalized and violent student agitation, after which the new front was forbidden to engage in any form of protest. In the same month, April 1968, certain municipalities were declared "doubtful" by the national security police, and, in July 1968, following the great protest of "one hundred thousand" in Rio, public demonstrations were forbidden. The Marcio Moreira Alves affair (Moreira Alves was a deputy accused of having insulted the armed forces) constituted the decisive event in the confrontation. In the face of Congressional refusal to waive the deputy's political immunity, the military in December 1968 suspended all representative assemblies. By Institutional Act No. 5, the president of the Republic was given almost unlimited power; within four months some 150 deputies or senators had been dismissed and numerous political rights had been suspended. The Federal Supreme Court was cut down in size and its powers reduced. All student leaders and almost a thousand additional students were arrested when the former National Union of Students held a clandestine meeting, and a systematic housecleaning was carried out in the universities.

In this climate of severe repression, clandestine and violent opposition came into being. Beginning in 1966 with bank robberies, the struggle continued in 1969 with a series of kidnappings, the first of which was the American ambassador. The semiemergency situation justified the new leadership in reinforcing the hard line. The 1967 Constitution was modified and the 1969 version included the recent articles and decrees placing power in the hands of the military. When President Costa e Silva fell ill, he was replaced by an officer, Garrasazu Medici, rather than by his legal civilian successor, Pedro Aleixo.

The political economy of these three presidential years was equally important in the establishment of the new regime. The rationalizing and reformist ideology of the military academy left its clear imprint on governmental action. After the housecleaning of Castelo Branco's government, a new development strategy inspired by a conception of rationalism and based on a neocapitalist model was undertaken by the new minister of development, Delfim Netto. At the urging of the minister of the interior, Alphonso Albuquerque Ilma, there commenced a new national era, a conquest of the Amazon. Economic progress became a first priority and a justification for the regime's existence: an example of its performance is shown in the fact that in 1970 inflation was contained at 22 percent and economic expansion reached 9.5 percent.

Spontaneous development and rationalized speedup of development

An hypothesis implicit in our analysis and in that of most Latin American specialists is that the change from populism to post-populism may be correlated with a change in the process of economic development and is accompanied by a modification of the economic policies adopted. In order to make the following chapters easier to understand, it would seem useful to define two points of economic evolution, spontaneous development and rationalized speedup of development. In the present work, each of these terms refers to a particular phase in the development process, to the particular economic policy adopted, and to the social and political strategy used to make that policy operative.

Spontaneous development

This phrase corresponds to that point in political development when populism has matured and begins its decline. It refers to the first period of the development process when the young state is seeking to free itself from the old colonial or neocolonial system of economic relations based on the export of primary goods. The changeover from the old to the new system begins with import substitution, by which the new state seeks, through its own industrialization, to end its dependence on external markets for manufactured goods. This phase is called "spontaneous" because its first appearance is not the result of explicit policy. It has usually resulted from some extraordinary event, such as the outbreak of a world war or the economic crisis of 1929, which reduced the possibility of imports or so inflated the national currency that the traditional exporting sector was handicapped. It continues to be spontaneous in its later development, because analysts believed at that time that the socioeconomic system could adapt in such a way as to pass spontaneously from its former state of dependence to that of self-sufficiency.

This optimistic vision shared by the "developmentalists" implies a certain stimulating role on the part of those in political power. The state provides that economic stimulation which seems appropriate at a given point, but its action is not laid down in a detailed and systematic program covering each stage of the development process.

The action is also intermittent because it tends to come at particular times when specific social gratifications are necessary. Long-term harmonious evolution is left to the internal mechanisms of the system, which in theory lead by themselves to the mobilization of different social groups and to their integration and participation at various levels of the social, economic, and political life of the country. While awaiting the final results of the process, those tensions born of change and the immediate demands and aspirations of particular groups will be relieved as a result of the process of continuous expansion. Drawing upon the resources provided by the new dynamic of development, an astute policy of resource allocation permits the satisfaction of immediately pressing claims as they are presented. The appearance of internal contradiction and conflict in the policy is put off into an indefinite future.

The government of Juscelino Kubitscheck (1956–1960) represented the apogee of this phase and of the developmentalist concept. Taking place in a climate of euphoria, the period was marked by a spontaneous mobilization around development projects, of which the establishment of Brasilia is a fine example. Later history appears to belie the validity of the optimistic vision of spontaneous development.

Rationalized speeding up of development

The change in regime appears to have corresponded to a change in the development process. The spontaneous mechanisms for "take off" were evidently not sufficient in themselves to create development. The "renewal of development" phase was thus derived from a period of decline in the development process and constituted a necessary stage in recovery which followed not a spontaneous course but one purposely designed to accompany an expression of the general political will.

The concept of development and the "rationalized" policy associated with this phase was virtually the reverse of the former populist model. The new power elite insisted on being "realistic." It believed in the expansion potential of the Brazilian economy, but insisted above all on the necessity of realizing the constraints to expansion. Inspired by neocapitalist thinking, the new model sought to restore the general play of normal economic mechanisms. Distribution of credit and profit were subordinated to progress in production and in productivity. Measures accompanying industrial expansion rested more on improvement of the economic environment—budgetary policy, monetary correction, minor devaluation—than on direct intervention. Less "nationalistic," the new elite placed Brazilian develop-

14

ment explicitly within the framework of the international economy. National and foreign capital was channeled into the most competitive industrial sectors, where capital intensive industrialization was practiced on a grand scale and where the state and multinational corporations played a major role.

The political and social strategy which accompanied this new model was totally contrary to the laissez-faire optimism of the preceding regime. As with economic development, social and political development had to be programmed. Although general satisfaction of all interests might be postulated for some indefinite future, it was seen to have little short-term value. Indeed, certain interests would have to be sacrificed for the sake of economic development priorities. Rather than responding immediately and constantly to all social demands, those in political power chose to scale the access of interest groups to the fruits of social and political advancement. Mobilization, integration, the ability to participate in the market economy, in the consuming society, and in public borrowing were progressive, each step forward being limited to specific groups, first directed toward workers in key industries in the urban sector, then toward workers in the rural areas most closely allied to the urban economy. This principle of "restricted mobilization" carries over to the political level as well. Communication between the leaders and the population was reduced very substantially, and the power to decide issues or to give advice was granted to only certain actors whose influence was, in any case, limited.

2 General framework

Differing forms of social confrontation, whether institutionalized or spontaneous, ranging from simple social pressures to the systematic use of violence, occur in the more advanced parts of contemporary Latin America. Our framework will be the authoritarian regimes, or governments of the power-elite, which followed in the midsixties the process of spontaneous development. Our model will be the military technocracy of Brazil which arose after the revolution of 1964 overthrew populism. Similarities to this model may be seen in the Argentinian regime after the fall of Illia in 1966 and more particularly during the Onganía and Levingston periods.

The new authoritarianism in Latin America is not merely a continuation of the continent's ever present, though ever changing, quota of governments which have broken with the formal democratic structure. Such regimes were necessary pawns in the operative framework of the semicolonial systems, in which the military would attempt to restore equilibrium by acting as arbiter within a never-ending rotation of oligarchies. In contemporary Latin America, however, seizure of power by the armed forces no longer derives solely from this background; now the armed forces have, for the first time, seized power simultaneously in the key countries of the continent.

The new authoritarianism presents certain specific characteristics: it is no longer a stage in the stagnant round of colonial politics; it marks, on the contrary, a stage in a dynamic process of social change. Our analysis, for example, does not apply to the Valasco Alvarado government of Peru. The really important point in defining the significance of the Brazilian and Argentinian regimes is that the armed forces played a role in the organization of these regimes and that the regimes result from expansion of systems of spontaneous development. These regimes have great importance because they have arisen in the most advanced socioeconomic systems of the continent. They are the last stage in a process of social change in Latin America which has produced, simultaneously, industrialization, urbanization, and the formation of internal markets. One might argue that the Peruvian regime should be regarded as a premature intervention by the mili-

16

tary in this process, but the Peruvian case does not present the same characteristics of exhausting the import-substitution model which characterized the accelerating process of social change in Brazil and Argentina. The importance of these technomilitary regimes is that they represent the most advanced point in the crisis of spontaneous development. In this sense, the technocratic-military regimes of Brazil and Argentina have inaugurated a model which is but one point in a curve, and which will probably be imitated by other nations which have not yet attained full maturity in the process of change. Starting with the characteristics of the Brazilian process, it may be possible to explain the correlation between the economic and political subsystems which form a part of the curve of change which has taken place in Latin America since 1945.

The presumed convergence of democracy and development

The possible dysfunctions which result from the confrontation between democracy and development are also the objects of our study. Since the halting forward steps and the backsliding of a democratic regime may be seen as a counterpart to the profound changes brought about by economic development, our study requires that every aspect we study of democratic political operation correspond to an analysis of per capita revenue, the expansion of internal markets or, indeed, to the differentiation and expansion through industrialization which characterize economic development. According to the conventional view of change, economic prosperity should increase the feeling of participation in the decision-making process and thus should reinforce the structures of representation and the diversity of interests which make up the "general will" of a nation; it should also help to create differentiations within the functions of power. This study maintains that the very concept of confrontation between democracy and development in countries at this stage of change in Latin America presumes the collapse of the normative characteristics common to a period of spontaneous development and that a well-defined phase in the expansion of economic, political, social, and cultural subsystems has already taken place.

The first hypothesis of our analysis is that the new regimes of Latin America are fundamentally different from previous military governments of "national salvation" (which were in power more or less temporarily), although this appeared to be the initial objective of the Castelo Branco administration. The very success of this administration led, however, to the downgrading of the democratic model. The life of this regime was extended, nevertheless, only with a "bad conscience" and led to a nostalgia for conventional legality as demonstrated by the Constitution of 1967. The internal logic of a reform program of development founded on neocapitalism put to the test the conventional view of the interconnection of spontaneous development and democracy. The new models may, in fact, be characterized by their abandonment of the hypothesis that economic change converges with the preservation of the traditional institutions of democratic regimes.

Any analysis of contemporary technocratic-military regimes which seeks to find in them a new model that will serve as a political counterpart to their economic ability to regain the momentum of development must address itself to one all-important question. To what degree and at what point, in the course of spontaneous development, have the mechanisms of democracy designed to recognize special interests and to conciliate divergent social aspirations really been put to the test? To what degree has there developed simultaneously with the growth of national prosperity a general will or a self-regulation of diverse interests? Any policy designed to regain development momentum must choose between clear alternatives and must evaluate costs and benefits.

The important question is to ascertain whether the political model adopted was indeed a necessary counterpart to economic policies already chosen. Did the period of spontaneous development establish a model that could reconcile the processes of economic and political development? Or, on the contrary, in this period when rational decision was most difficult and the greatest diversity of options was possible, did the economic and political subsystems in fact fail to converge.

18

Democratization and decompression

After ten years of technocratic-military regimes, hopes for continued progress toward the restoration of conventional democracy in Brazil have gradually disappeared. However, efforts to find new political structures which would correspond to the self-sufficiency and speed of development shown by the economic model continued. Analysis of the struggle for new political forms becomes even more complex if one adds to it the aspirations for redemocratization.

The analysis must also make a model that is workable; in so doing it will be found that the model differs substantially from the "decompression" model envisioned by some political scientists. The decompression model is designed to compensate in the long term for the consolidation that the authoritarian regimes have introduced into the process of social change in Latin America. Based on a notion that a universal model of democracy appears and disappears, the decompression model seems to neglect the role of resentment in the political reality of these regimes. But it does not presuppose a circular model, which preserves traditional "legality" and the democratic formula as well as military intervention. In Brazil in 1964 economic change led to the search for a formula of "consensus" democracy as opposed to previous "general will" models. In a consensus democracy dissent undergoes a qualitative change of expression in the play between immediate necessity and the long-range aspiration for a continuity of economic development. Confrontation becomes increasingly radical in an attempt to break down a system which by its very nature inhibits the traditional activity of opposition in the classic structure of the legislative assembly.

Our analysis centers on the search for a typology of political confrontation, ranging from mild forms of protest to the naked play of pressure groups acting directly against the center of established power and seeking to overthrow it. In their search for a new institutional form, the post-1964 Brazilian and Argentine governments moved in a direction that all countries do when the process of social change conflicts with basic political and economic aspirations. The effort toward continued development—expressed as an elementary desire to escape stagnation—brings about a basic political realignment.

Some may see in this a kind of "retrocession" in the development process that brings the Latin-American countries to the same level of interplay between economic and political forces that are to be seen in the Afro-Asian countries in their break with the old colonial order. The new "relaunching" of Brazil and Argentina in the sixties stems from a basic demand to escape from inertia. Although the greater class differentiation among Latin-American countries allowed more refinement of demands, the politics of post-spontaneous development are based on the same urge toward "social mobilization" that prompted the seizure of the economic structures of the old order or the building of national single parties in the young Afro-American states. It is with this new and more elemental level of political realignment that Brazil and Argentina paid the price of wasting the opportunities created by the spontaneous phase of development. With it the convergence of democracy and development has disappeared.

Populism: allocation of resources replaces the mechanisms of pluralist negotiation

The irreversible trend toward technocratic-military regimes might be defined historically as the end of populism. The structural changes precipitated by conditions after 1945 made possible the beginning of social changes both in Brazil and Argentina without ever having put to the test the bargaining and pressure mechanisms social groups and classes possessed. Had this taken place, we might be able to talk of a synthesis of aspirations based on the general will and on democracy. In the period of spontaneous development, no effective confrontation in social demands appeared, for the state assumed the position of arbitrator. It directed the distribution of benefits, as well as giving definition to the aspirations for social change, and adopted policies the sole purpose of which was clearly to assist specific groups.

Latin American populism (particularly that of Brazil) sought to substitute for the dynamic process of social demands and collective pressures the extended use of state mechanisms for resource allocation. The fact that the working class had obtained favorable social legislation without recourse to a general strike clearly points to the weakening, in Third World social and political evolution, of the reciprocity and bargaining which are the bases of the democratic model. Populism benefited from strategies of resource allocation and from a development policy which replaced bargaining mechanisms with general economic advances in society. It goes without saying that the benefits received by certain groups and classes in this arbitrary redistribution of resources did not correlate with their actual pressure or bargaining power. Only state control of the rate of social change could create equilibrium between the upper and lower social levels in the community. The administration became a prisoner of its own manipulations, through the underutilization of state power and through the reversal of dependency relations within a patronage society. It is important to underline that populism's utilization of statutory regulation had a decisive effect on social mobility within the country.

From this statutory foundation arose the mechanisms of assistance by which the state directed the process of change in Brazil, independent of the relative strength of the actors on the stage. An example of this is the minimum wage legislation that became necessary as a result of the expansion of the internal market and of the industrial sector. A further example may be found in the manipulation of international currencies for the benefit of the growing national bourgeoisie. Unfortunately this manipulation failed to take into account that increased productivity was necessary to accelerate the process of import substitution. Regardless of the dynamics of the forces at play, the transfer of resources from the export economy into the internal market sector was not foreseen. All of these processes are typical of the recent experience of developing countries. In none of these processes is it possible to discover any relationship between economic interests and democratic political structures or between the pressures and counterpressures of the reciprocal elements constituting the interplay between state and society. Out of this situation has arisen an omnipresent state whose relationship to the society is totally ambiguous. This ambiguity allows the state to avoid the confrontation which would have truly tested whether the democratic system had indeed been institutionalized. During the period of spontaneous development, conflict between workers and management never really revealed the forces involved and never really came to grips with the power relationships which had been so radically altered from those pertaining in Brazilian society prior to the fifties.

The ambiguity in the system

The entire system has never tested the real limits of its institutional flexibility or of its tolerance of confrontation. The period of spontaneous development came into being with a low level of social coercion; the state continued to follow the rules of the game of electoral succession and the different branches of government remained independent. Military groups were penetrated by legalistic ideologies, as opposed to the overall ideology of "national salvation" that was typical of the oligarchies of the old regime. Populism flourished as a result of the policy of governmental assistance, which rapidly became a policy of munificence.

The natural improvement of the position of all groups as a result of this first stage of change ostensibly relieved the state of its function as arbitrator, but the system made the holders of power susceptible to a latent type of Bonapartism: that is, a succession of regimes which gave each class of society—classes which themselves derived from spontaneous development—advantages, then took them away. Clearly the model of a bargaining democracy becomes obsolete in a society that does not allow expression of its own internal tensions.

The continuous revision of class position as a result of the redistribution of national income concealed the slowing down of the expansion of real production. Moreover the system of subsidies concealed, in fact, the real competition between economic groups, which could no longer count on continued economic expansion to eliminate the contradictions within the system. Inflation permitted continuous and automatic rise in subsidies but, thanks to this compensation between spiraling costs and prices, a momentary truce was gained among the actors on the social stage during the spontaneous change period in the fifties.

The climax of the spontaneous development period was marked not only by the relaxation of demands made by the social groups and

22

classes but also, because of this, by a decline in the possibility of bargaining or democratic negotiation. Characteristic of this phase, too, was the ostensible redistribution of wealth which came from systematic inflation and the generalized crisis which the continued existence of the system as a whole generated. In addition to the profound social erosion which these factors created, the ambiguous role of governmental control resulted in a final state of crisis that turned the state upon itself in a never-ending reallocation of resources. The apparatus of government lost, in consequence, its capacity to lead the development process or to maintain an effective reserve of power and decision.

Social erosion and the emptiness of power

It is not surprising, then, that the final stages of populism clearly display the political struggle between the positive left and the negative left, as the Brazilian situation in 1962 demonstrated. The two lefts represent antagonistic strategies to give consistency to state action and to reorganize a nucleus of national decision-making after the mechanisms of subvention destroy government effectiveness. Every attempt to recoup the situation, however, requires radical state action in order to assure the existence of a coherent regime, whether socialist or not. The state must be able to turn collective aspirations away from the complacent relaxation to which inflation has raised them, while at the same time retaining an ostensibly democratic framework.

The system of resource allocation had made possible the innocent interplay of irreconcilable demands. The almost instantaneous consolidation of the technocratic-military system in Brazil derived in part from the power vacuum that erosion of the process of social stratification had created. The regime enjoyed broad maneuverability in locating a new center of social decision making. Its greatest asset at the outset, was a high degree of ideological coherence.

It is rare to find a high degree of agreement between the actual effect of a political system on society and the doctrine which determines its action. But this close correlation did exist between the doctrine the War College espoused and the way the intellectual aristocracy

of the Brazilian army exercised power during the government of
Castelo Branco. From the very first, this cohesion between the theore-
ticians and the practitioners gave the new regime an increasing ability
to innovate; it could and did subordinate the building of a political
model to a new style of state intervention into the realities of society.
It permitted the administration that came into being in 1964 to go
beyond, in its organization of power, the instinctive resistance to the
conventional democratic view of the political system held by the first
leaders of the movement.

Rationalizing change: the search for a consensus

The strongest characteristic of the new regime was its ability to eliminate ambiguity within the Brazilian state through the articulation of
a neocapitalist model for development that replaced the lack of solid
structure during the period of spontaneity by a new kind of programmatic integration and a new play of alternatives. Its first impact on
the political subsystem was to eliminate the superstructure of
bargaining and the process of formulation of the general will within
groups and classes. This approach, widely advertised as consensus democracy, presupposed the systematic suppression of certain types of
political actors (by the elimination of their political rights), the
urgent redefinition of values to be sought in social change (a redefinition made compulsory by striking down, as subversive, projects
which differed from those of the chosen order), and the imposition of
limitations on intermediary groups (such as trade unions), which the
rigor of the new economic model made necessary.

Between 1945 and the present, then, the political system has
changed from a regime of conciliation with no real confrontation to a
structure in which rigidly defined social aspirations are determined by
establishing a coherent political program and by a broad acceptance of
the social and economic costs of this program. The principle of social
consensus and the hypothesis that the grand strategy of the regime
would eventually satisfy the aspirations of every social group were
thus introduced into the heart of the political system. The idea of the
rationality of consensus derives from the social origin of the new

holders of power. It was drawn from the ideology of the middle class of the military and from the liberal tendencies of the technocrats, who were allied neither to the traditional structure of power of the oligarchic regimes nor to the industrial bourgeoisie which had been favored at the stage of spontaneous development.

A first rule concerning divergence from the consensus was early established. At the center of the power structure, divergence from a consensus decision might be accepted, but within narrow limits. That is to say, debate deriving from a special subtlety of point of view might be allowed to change minor aspects of action, but divergence would be acceptable only on the premise that tolerance must not appear to the technocrats as irrational or scientifically inconsistent. Clearly, any divergent viewpoint should concern simply the methods of execution of a project or relate to purely marginal aspects of the new, rigid policy of development.

Postpopulism—from trophic to dystrophic development

Thus we find that in 1964 not only was a new economic structure adopted, but the formal aspects of the preceding political system were eliminated. The Brazilian populism of Juscelino Kubitschek and the creative phase of Péronism seemed to provide empirical support for the thesis of the coexistence of economic development and conventional democracy, but neither system gave real verification of an interdependent relationship between the two.

The period beginning in 1964 was characterized by the adoption of a dystrophic model of social change. This expression is related to the concept of "trophos," or balanced progression, within an ordered process of social evolution. This coordinated process involves all changes in the economic, political, social, and cultural subsystems to the degree that they tend to move in one direction of cumulative reaction, thus allowing the system in its totality to benefit from harmonious exchanges. The dystrophic model favors social differentiation and complexity.

It is not our task here to discuss the empirical validity of the hypothesis of trophic development, but the preceding paragraphs have sought to demonstrate that this model of change would be limited in its application to a period of spontaneous development. Whatever its actual value, the trophic model was widely accepted by the pre-1964 theory of development. Today, when the dimensions of the confrontation going on within this policy of rational change are evident, it is clear that this concept is dysfunctional to an effective and dialectically satisfactory policy of political development. The concept leaves intact the *theoretical* possibility of reconciling different economic and political systems but collapses when, with the passing of spontaneity, the truce in the interplay of aspirations in the social classes affected by change disappears.

Compensation and complementarity between subsystems

The system of dystrophic change characterizes the postspontaneous period and is associated with authoritarian systems of change. The increase in gross national product, in per capita income, and in the average wage is exchanged for the collapse of political representation. Pluralism is eliminated from the decision-making process. In the postspontaneous period benefits limited to certain groups of the population may well result from the continued process of change, but this is in contradistinction to the general system mobilization under rational development and to the radical absorption of the subsistence sector by the market-economy sector. Dystrophic development abandons the political and economic indications which had been essential to measuring performance (i.e., higher per capita income leading to broader political representation). The rate and locus of change is not parallel in all systems. The two systems are often characterized by stages of disequilibrium in which an area undergoing essential change will take in all the others. Evidence of economic success at any given point will correspond to the system's capacity to absorb the totality of demands made on it. It is not necessary to examine exhaustively the different types of crises which arise in the course of the process of change. The essential point is to consider the scale of priorities which determine the type of response the regime will make—priorities which condition total social demand. At different times there will be subsystems within which the effects of change may be concentrated and these will, in turn, satisfy the demands of other subsystems.

During the stage of rational development, according to the dystrophic model of change, the authoritarian technocracy's consolidation of the consensus policy includes: a) a compensatory mechanism which permits the *economic* subsystem to respond to the differentiated demands made in the political system (this mechanism may derive entirely from the various allocatory strategies created for any desired division of advantages and sacrifices); and b) the crystalization of consensus into an objective plan of social change which presupposes, ideally, the reconciliation of all groups and interests, thus preventing the rise of competitive structures that might in turn affect the center of power. The reinforcement and eventual expansion of the regime implies not the reinstallation of conventional democracy but the pursuit of the real requirements of differentiation within the system, which result from the dialectic of the allocation of resources and the vicissitudes of "consensus."

The significance of confrontation

Confrontation in Latin America does not seek to determine the content of change; rather, it offers total opposition to the consensus which is supposed to underlie the dystrophic model of social change.

Historically, confrontation has opposed the governments of power elites, such as military-technocracies. Confrontation has also presupposed certain premises of political institutionalization that have been abolished by the consensual model. In attempting to prove that the conventional democratic model is a necessary consequence of economic development neither supporters or critics of the technocratic system find outlets for the tensions characteristic of the dystrophic process of change. The result is a classic vicious circle of aggravated confrontation.

Generalized confrontation is thus structurally limited by the necessity to create compensatory relationships within different social subsystems. The actors in the confrontation are structurally discrete groups. The study of confrontation in Latin America cannot, in fact, be examined from the viewpoint of the potential spread of these structurally separated groups; nor can it be judged by the capacity of social classes or groups to make evident their dissent. This study considers not only the form of confrontation but also the actors in it, who are linked by socially determined, noninterchangeable roles. Dissent in a dystrophic development model cannot be envisaged as operating continuously. It does not occur as it does, according to traditional analysis, in other great polities of the world. It does not correspond to the classical avant-garde socialist position. Instead there are in Latin America today groups which might be called the "unpunishables," white-collar workers, students, and intellectuals, whose activities are symbolic rather than being directed toward the spread of social dissent. These groups may turn to "physical" activity, which may become more and more violent, but they show few signs of effective intervention; in other words, there is little hope that they will find real social integration for their own "countercultures."

Anomie and institutionalization

An additional characteristic of current Latin American confrontation is the particular form it takes given the specific social conflicts it reacts to and given the roles played by escalation and institutionalization in the confrontation process. Those who engage in confrontation present an entire spectrum of oppressed groups, which share at least one characteristic—declining claim to the exercise of power. Contemporary confrontation destroys parliament's presumed role and it institutionalizes violence because the established power in society has lost the monopoly of legitimacy. The escalation of confrontation has, however, nothing of *anomie* about it. Each stage in the process requires fresh negotiations among the groups concerned as well as a reevaluation of the instruments of pressure. Rules of the game tend to be established. Because escalation is a slow process, a rich diversity has appeared in the forms of Latin American confrontation. Varying levels of violence are utilized and a code of confrontation has crystallized to different degrees.

The predisposition to suspend hostilities and to seek negotiation is evidence of a preference for the bargaining which has been effectively eliminated by adoption of the consensual model. Thus, any attempt to classify the stages of recourse to violence will reflect a growing antithesis between the possibilities of conciliation offered by the technocratic system and the ever more differentiated interests and aspirations in the society. At the same time, there is a great possibility of institutionalization at each of these stages, in view of the slippage between threatened violence and the real intention to engage in violence on the part of the actors.

Escalation and radicalization

There exists then, simultaneously with the tendency toward violence, a continuous presupposition of compatibility at the base of the confrontation. In escalation there is always an aspect of frustrated negotiation and confrontation retains the germ of the conciliation mechanisms which the period of spontaneous development created. That is why every confrontation vacillates, displaying the stop-and-go characteristics, in which it first radicalizes conflict and then declares a truce.

But the effect on the potential institutionalizing of violent dissent engendered by combining a dystrophic state of change with the consensual model of political organization cannot be denied. And if the descent into violence is slow, it is nonetheless irremediable. Any attempt by the established power to create an underlying concensus deeply affronts the dissidents; conversely, the slightest dissident pressure causes a corresponding degree of repression. This is the origin of the concept of "deterrence"; by the total deployment of the coercive apparatus at the slightest provocation, society is reminded of the hegemony of those who hold social control.

In essence, there is no turning back in the escalation of confrontation. The positions of the actors are not symmetrical or equal in deciding the level of conflict; the regime maintains a sufficiently rigid response so that the dissidents can set the level of violence. If those engaging in confrontation have enough initiative to mount a challenge, the government simply has no alternative but to match in degree and in intensity the pressure exerted against established power.

Once unleashed, active confrontation can no longer be contained. There can be no expectation of one side responding in a way which might reconcile the dissidents with those who seek to maintain the *status quo*. Only by reformulating the political model and hence by finding a new basis of legitimacy can normalization of the institutional mechanism take place so that the marginal sectors of society may be absorbed.

Taming dissent once unleashed presupposes a recognition of the entire political structure. In its slow development, dissent indicates initially a profound upsetting of the social stabililty that is based upon the credibility of formal authority. The whole panoply of stages by which the confrontation reaches the limit of radical antagonism must be studied.

It must be admitted that the trend toward even greater disruption brought on by the present pattern of nationalized development in Argentina and Brazil is leading slowly toward a point of no return. Although the present widespread confrontation is unable to produce a dramatic change in the power structure, it nevertheless points up the pitfalls that must be avoided on the hard road to any future reconciliation. The unprecedented peaks of tension revealed in violent protest bear little resemblance to a classic program of democratic restoration.

The Argentine situation of July 1973 shows this clearly. Full resumption of a democratic regime did not lead to the social truce demanded by Héctor Cámpora that had been made all the more necessary by the return of Péron to power. The contesting forces did not allow a full airing of all the different radical viewpoints which had developed throughout the technocratic-military regime. Decompression did not result in the laying down of arms but in a confrontation between the judicialists and the socialists, who were themselves a product of divided Péronism. The political prisons were emptied by the new regime without the ERP (the Popular Revolutionary Army), and the Montoneros becoming integrated into the Popular Front, made possible by General Lanusse's Great Reconciliation Pact. Redemocratization faced tough and determined actions, convinced of the necessity to impress on the social fabric their vision of change which had been concealed during the period of a power-elite system. The sudden abolition of the *régime d'exception* only served to stimulate the appearance of urban forces which were, for the first time, able to express a free opinion.

3 The gap between development and democracy

The study of the types of confrontation created by the present experience of development in Latin America must be placed in a specific historical setting—that is, at the stage of decline in the spontaneous transformation of the so-called "colonial" situation—the period which following the Second World War that was the height of the populist regimes. The technocratic breakthrough coincided with the exhaustion of the process of import substitution and the crises that slowed down the rate of growth in the late fifties. The effort to regain development was thereupon directed toward instituting highly rationalized programs of development which strongly emphasize planning while remaining compatible with a basically neocapitalist model. The political counterpart of this was the "power-elite" government,[1] characterized, though in different proportions, by the allocation of the power of decision-making to the military and civil technocracy—two groups which until that time had remained marginal to the traditional mechanisms of popular representation. These regimes emerged when it became evident that in addition to the acute deterioration of external commercial trade terms, society was suffering acute erosion. This had been brought about by the inflationary mechanisms these new populist regimes had adopted at first as a calculated risk, in order to assure continuous industrialization as well as the effective establishment of a long-term model of self-sufficient development.[2]

We do not yet have sufficient historical perspective to know whether the passing of the spontaneous development period will put an end to the basic premise of systemic development, namely, that development is a synchronized and symmetrical process in which each sector undergoes changes in the same degree, and according to the same standards or in the same directions, as all other sectors. The ultimate meaning of development under this earlier formulation—so to speak, its macrosocial significance—would simply be the total sum of the changes within each subsystem that had taken place according to a parallel evolution, in terms both of differentiation and self-reliance.

It might be heuristically suggested that once the process of import substitution had been exhausted, as in the Brazilian case, and once the economic subsystems had realized their possibilities as mechanisms to bring about self-imposed social change, the delays and the problems presented in the course of development would have eliminated the presupposition of simultaneity.[3] Continuing development efforts rely heavily on planning and necessarily upon development of a middle- or long-term nature. The correlation between promotion of new development systems and the consolidation of the power-elite political system becomes clearer as the present authoritarian regimes can no longer be considered the result of emergency situations or as prologues to civilian governments and to conventional forms of popular representation.

The confrontation between developing and affluent societies

Because of the close correlation between the power-elite regimes and the neocapitalist development model, the phenomenon of confrontation or manifestation of dissent in countries such as Brazil and the Argentine is not a simple reflection of the dissent which has appeared in developed western societies. Analysis, for example, of France in May 1968 or of the rebellion on American campuses or of the "hard hat" movement shows that these crises have already, according to the Almond and Pye model,[4] been resolved in large measure by a greater redistribution of social wealth.

Confrontation in Latin America is fundamentally different from that in societies of abundance; its sociological roots lie in traditional anarchism.[5] The episodes of confrontation in the past two centuries have in reality been a quest for the ultimate framework within which the final confrontation might take place.[6] Since the developed societies have already achieved systemic integration, any critique of their intrinsic legitimacy became essentially a challenge of the *status quo* and of the establishment itself. Any approach to the phenomenon of confrontation must be related to the point in time (in terms of the development spectrum) at which it takes place. This study is concerned with confrontation at just one phase of change, the period at which, for the first time, the contradictions in the process of growth challenge the assumption of convergence between the benefits and costs of development.

Other societies, such as Brazil and Argentina today, are characterized by a dystrophic [7] development model, in which the levels of development attained by their economic subsystems have led, in the political subsystem, to the new regimes of the power elite. It is too soon to see the ultimate consequences of the spontaneous development period; we do not know yet whether the break in the ideally symmetrical relationship between economic development and democracy may signify a new phase in the process of social change.[8] Instruments of coercion may be used to mobilize the nation in order to maximize the increasingly rare opportunities to resuscitate the previous development program. Then again, it may be that, having exhausted the possibilities of the postwar period, we are present, in effect, at the structural death of the opportunity for social change in the Third World. Or it may be that the emergence of fully developed nation-states may no longer be possible in today's framework of international forces.[9]

The framework of confrontation:
emergence of the power elite systems

These new types of confrontation are directly related to the appearance of political regimes which can be characterized thus:

1. Within the economic subsystem
    a) They have adopted a clearly reformist attitude and seek to eliminate obsolete systems of production.
    b) They have concentrated on a localized redistribution of income, principally through the effective collection of taxes and by the constant improvement of the average minimum wage in the sectors already incorporated into the market economy.[10]
    c) They have chosen a system of high concentration on industry by altering their economies of scale. They have also sought

34

to integrate, through planning and controls, the public and private sectors into a new industrial whole for the country.[11]

2. In the political subsystem

   a) They have changed the meaning of representation in the organization of political parties.[12] In Brazil, for example, they have established and now control a two-party system in which one party plays the "establishment" and the other the "opposition." [13]

   b) They have reduced the margin of electoral choice by limiting the number of candidates and by controlling the selection of candidates at all levels.

   c) They have reduced the pluralist connotation implicit in federal organization (federations, states, municipalities) by enlarging the sphere of central power at the expense of state and municipal governments.[14]

   d) They have reduced the level of autonomy and increased the interdependence of the functions of power by absorbing into the executive a large part of the competence and control which had hitherto been reserved to the judicial and the legislative branches.

   e) Finally, within the political system they have reduced the interaction between the actors in the system and public opinion by establishing direct or indirect governmental censorship and by creating mechanisms of self-censorship within the media.

An overview view of the evolution and the consolidation of this system may be sketched as follows:

Generalized aspirations for systemic benefits

In a population which already enjoys a market economy, there exists a clear tendency to generalize the advantages of development. A convergence is created between the status quo attained by the new policy of development and the average level of aspiration created within the community by the process of change. This congruence may be further reinforced by certain general governmental budgetary polices [15]—i.e., by immediate statutory modification of the national revenue. Such modification may include precise and localized definition of revenue sources among certain social sectors or classes. Contrary to what happened in the fifties, governmental intervention today is no longer restricted to the field of production; government acts directly on the distribution of revenue in order to improve conditions of the consumer market. These new conditions are reflected in higher return from the productive sector and encouragement toward reinvestment, particularly of social overhead investment within the general framework of governmental policy (in education, health, or housing).

Increasing dependence on the political as opposed to the economic

The more economic performance improves, the more political activity will be conditioned by the functional requirements of the developmental apparatus. [16] Indeed, as Apter has suggested, the political subsystem becomes a dependent variable when the economy is sufficiently industrialized. From this point of view, it would not be difficult to create the permanent mechanisms of centralization required for planning (although the price for this may well be the destruction of previous models of decentralization, such as the Latin American federal state) or to have the executive and the legislature define the boundaries of the public sector of the national economy by utilizing mechanisms of budgetary allocation and execution. The predominance of centralization in political systems where there exists the influence of a political and institutional counterpart to development in the economic sphere tends to obscure aspects that characterized the former political subsystem. Political mobilization or participation, for example, are relegated to the level of latent activity. It is not simply a question of establishing that, historically, improved performance in the economic system has been followed by increasing modification of the political system. One premise of the classic functionalist scheme is that modifications in the political system *necessarily* correspond to the effects of progressive differentiation and autonomy in an economic system that defines development as "modernization" of the former colonial societies. The recent evolution of Latin America shows how a new and strongly imposed model of development can upset previous assumptions about patterns of change.[17]

It is not simply a question of analyzing the post-1960 constitutions in Latin America. The new institutions of these power-elite regimes have already gone beyond the former ideals of conventional political progress, such as those still to be found, for example, in the Punta del Este Charter and in Title X of the Foreign Assistance Act of 1968. It is time to admit that delay between stages of economic progress and political participation is normal.[18] The essential point is to recognize what institutional responses should be made to political demands at any given time; perhaps one response to dissent should be to allow at least symbolic expression of it.

The relative tolerance of dissent on the part of certain groups, such as students, the clergy, and a part of the intellectual elite may be interpreted as a tactical move aimed at tying symbolically the aspiration for political expression to the least dangerous groups in society. By choosing as "privileged antagonists" those minority groups which have little connection to social class (and hence are incapable of infecting society with their social conscience), the regime can channel reform demands into a cul-de-sac.[19] These "socially unpunishable" groups serve to compensate for the failure of the political system to promote fundamental change.

Participation as an exchange for resource allocation

In the degree to which a program for continuing development is actually executed, the model, as well as the crisis points, of change are also modified.[20] In effect, continuing development does not imply that there will be found initially a social continuum into which it can be placed. A new order of causation occurs, which may lead, for example, to the reopening of crises once resolved in the course of the spontaneous development phase. A crisis of participation may appear, for example, where, through a new policy of income allocation,[21] government concedes, by preferential statute, certain advantages to be derived from development in exchange for the recipients giving up wider access to the national decision-making power.[22] The process of development and its eventual success makes possible the creation of residual areas of dissent which differ from those deriving simply from a linear succession of crises, such as that suggested by the Almond/Pye model. The new development policies follow highly rational models, generally very different from those of the spontaneous development phase. The present period of change is the result of a series of complex historical factors, in which are combined the previous tendency toward cyclical crises and an ability to accept unexpected social movements that were not part of the original challenge of development. Table 1 (p. 39) shows the evolution of development crises in Brazil 1964 and the stages achieved under each president.

Dissent and confrontation in the different phases of development

In the developing countries of Africa and Asia, the first flush of spontaneous development was accompanied by an intense degree of national mobilization. Development became a real "paraideology"; [23] it mobilized the most diverse social classes because they were unified in oppposing the declining colonial society and favored an industrial society.[24]

The feeling of collective identity was not a simple recognition of a common cultural background; it also expressed a common view of national goals which included a consensus about the desirability of development.[25] The Musjarawa or Mufakat in Indonesia,[26] for example, represent perhaps the most advanced form of institutionalizing group and class adherence to a program of change expressed as nationalist development.[27] This mechanism parallels the single or dominant parties found in the Afro-Asian countries and is identified with the paraideological character of this specific type of nationalism. This kind of national institution also affects the formation of a collective will in the Third World.

Table 1

The crises of development in technocratic scheme
confrontation with the Almond/Pye model
(as applied to the Brazilian experience)

	Almond/Pye Model	Technocratic-Authoritarian Model	Problems	
Phases	Penetration	Penetration or Centralization	Integrated organization of the governmental machine	
	Integration	Integration	Breakdown of fiscal clientalism	Castello Branco Government
			Implanting of a bureaucratic machine	
			Regional and national planning	
			National communications systems	Costa E Silva Government
	Participation	Identity	Formulation of a development consensus	Medici Government
			Symbols of mobilization	
	Identity	Legitimacy	Institutionalization of dissent	
	Legitimacy	Participation	Extension of access to the mechanisms of allocation and decision	
	Distribution	Distribution	Correction of inequalities of access to the mechanisms of allocation and distribution	

Phases

The special case of Latin America

Insofar as Latin America is concerned, the attempt to direct the body politic toward national consensus within the classic formulas of political alignment was unsuccessful. The single party does not characterize this period. The idea of forced institutional mobilization under the aegis of the executive was seen as a temporary aberration from conventional democracy.[28] Even as the power elite was determining new policies for controlling the mobilization of society, the Brazilian constitution of 1967 still retained declarations of pious intention, as well as the constitutional apparatus suitable to Western-style democracy and to the rules of negotiation among pressure groups, who were themselves the products of the traditional framework of regional and national assemblies.

The old populist model was committed to the democratic model in the strict sense of carrying on negotiations leading to the formulation of a "general will." [29] All the subsidiary aspects of democracy were untouched, including the complete absence of censorship, and the proscription of political crimes. The picture the power elite presented of spontaneous development was that of consensual mobilization for successful economic development and the preservation of the democratic model on the political front. Based on the expansion of vertical and horizontal mobility within democratic norms, the new model was identified with the rise of a local intelligentsia and with the affirmation of national self-determination.

In the process of introducing its development program, the populist regime preserved consensus and avoided dissent more by a conciliatory policy of resource allocation than by the conventional mechanisms of pluralistic bargaining.[30] It would be easy to express, in a succession of "time series," the compromises by which the official policy of development: a) counteracted the aspirations of dissenting classes and groups, b) alternated confiscation in the foreign sector with redistribution of internal income, particularly through minimum wage policies, c) compensated selected credit sources by market protection, d) favored, by customs protection, obsolete industrial complexes and stimulated concentration, and e) created a giant, but simultaneously timid, system of state economic intervention.[31] The result was to extend the links between the governmental development plan and those social groups who saw development as a form of paraideology, thus leaving the road open for a variety of expressions of dissent.[32]

The Exacerbation of Dissent

As the new development program progressed, the government of the power elite was able to break down the deep social *anomie* with which the period of spontaneous development had ended. Gone was the general ambiguity created by the institutional flexibility in which the great changes of the fifties had taken place. The exercise of power was now assigned exclusively to the armed forces, aided by a civil technocracy incorporated into a very highly formal structure of governance.[33] Successful development was predicated on employing the neocapitalist model. Government was preoccupied with optimal performance as well as with widespread social reform. To accomplish these goals a single, neutral protagonist was required to direct the entire process of change.

According to the new premises accepted by the power elite, "consensus" was demonstrated by the very rationality of the new national development plan. As the details of the plan became more concrete, however, the search for "consensus" tended to undermine any effort at long-term planning. The attempt to introduce a unified national purpose inevitably assumed a calculated risk of a clash with those groups and classes in society whose interests would ultimately be affected by the difficult adjustments in the system of production required for the success of the plan.

In short, the new regime tried to make dissent through confrontation less viable by emphasizing the extreme rationality of its actions, and for this reason perceived all opposition as simply an expression of personal, group, or class interest. They foresaw that the dissenters would inevitably be absorbed into the new structure.[34] The presupposition of instant and total response to popular demands current in the phase of spontaneous development was definitively eliminated. If identity between development and the general will were to be maintained, any short-range presupposition that economic progress would be compatible with any particular aspirations for social progress must disappear.

Under the new technocratic-military regime, dissent was manifested less as opposition to a specific development project than as a rejection of the entire new model of social change. In the flexible years of the fifties political ideals had more or less coincided with conventional notions of democratic representation, and economic performance was tied to the individualism that this type of political structure represented. With the new power-elite regimes the planning model created a complete break with these former ideals and dissent began to play a reverse role from that which it played under a democratic system in that it was no longer a right within the system but tended toward a complete rejection of the entire power-elite model.[35]

Necessarily, the close ideological homogeneity imposed on national policy and the presumption of consensus that it claimed to incorporate resulted in the elimination of alternatives, not only of a thematic order, but even more of a procedural order.[36]

Any rationalizing force that intervenes in the social process, claiming to have cured the defects of the past even at the cost of overthrowing an ostensibly legitimate government, immediately faces the necessity of consolidating its power in two fundamental ways:

   a) It must introduce a model of development that possesses a high degree of dogmatic consistency.

   b) It must provide an increasingly precise clarification of those actions which constitute confrontation.

Confrontation at this point tends to be defined by those in power as a manifestation of subversion and hence as a danger to the system as a whole.

The internal drive for a single systemic goal tends to make the regime apply international ideological terminology to the national situration. Internal social conflicts can then be labeled manifestations of a "revolutionary war," which means that national security and public safety must be redefined in terms of security against any sort of internal attack from any quarter.

National development planning under such circumstances becomes directly related to the suppression of popular dissent. The more successful the plan, the less there should be a need for repression. But in Latin America a more dynamic economic performance as a result of renewed development has produced no greater openness or tolerance of opposition in the dominant political forces. The hopes of the "progressives" of the sixties were destroyed. The exercise of the right to dissent was instead blocked by the very success of the new development policy.

The fact that antagonism to the plan did exist and that it was directed toward the new regime, meant that government policy, to be successful, required a high degree of ideological homogeneity. The operation of government also required exceptionally efficient organization in order to produce the results expected of the new development plan.[37]

Parameters of dissent in power-elite regimes

The more highly integrated the program of a new political and social order, the more incapable it is of using a flexible model of governmental action, in which determinative aspects can be negotiated in order to accommodate interests outside normal policy limits. Within these limits, the power-elite system will, in any case, tolerate a certain expression of difference by accepting, for example, discrete variations of official policy, so long as these are based on the same type of rationalism as that espoused by government and so long as discussion takes place within an institutional, not a political, framework. This, then, is what Apter meant when, as part of a nonrepresentative theory of participation,[38] he proposed a technocratic chamber. In the Brazilian experience, it is important to note that the power elite model gave birth to CONSPLAN (National Planning Council) in 1964 in order to assure, at the technocratic level, that representatives of the different socioeconomic sectors concerned with the process of national change would discuss the premises of the planning model. CONSPLAN parallels the Communal Provincial Councils established during Ongania's first regime in Argentina. Formerly this type of participation had permitted, at the regional level, a certain openness of debate on the criteria of planning.

However, at the level of general strategy, power-elite regimes have strongly resisted any expression of dissent. A perfect illustration of this particular rigidity, as we have already noted, is the way in which the apparatus of coercion in these regimes uses the concept of subversion. They permit some dissent, but always within very narrow limits. The power-elite system rejects all bloc opposition or opposition based on principle; it will not tolerate any criticism of the criteria chosen to promote interaction between the economic, political, social, and cultural subsystems of the community.[39] As is the case with any development policy, an effort at total reconstruction presupposes a point of departure and the making of choices. These choices will be both discretionary, and at the same time, irrevocable, so the discussion or adoption of any one alternative is a hindrance to the founding of a new social order. At that point suppression of dissent can be faced squarely, as also can the establishment of progressive deviation from the conventional framework of legitimacy. This is especially true in the efforts to harmonize the economic model with political aspirations.

By demanding that a return to democratic norms follow economic improvement, the dissenters touch on a sensitive point—the exclusive competence of those in power to define the agenda for change. It is this demand that defines the line between subversion and acceptable disagreement; at this point confrontation goes beyond the institutional framework to take the form of clandestine violence.

This kind of dissent cannot be accepted within the power-elite system because the domain of legal dissent has narrowed as the institutional structure of the regime has rigidified. Superinstitutionalization on one side creates equal and symmetrical poles of antagonism within the radical organization. Dissent becomes no longer merely protest; there grows up an effective interplay of bargaining and negotiation between two organized groups, and thus the radicals and the government discover an unexpected means of communication. New mechanisms of confrontation with the establishment take surprising forms. One of the clearest examples may be seen in the practice of political kidnapping.

Confrontation within power-elite regimes

Let us first establish several fundamental concepts. In these regimes confrontation means the collective expression of dissent. Dissent arises because a group or individual cannot satisfy its aspirations within the normal institutional mechanisms. Confrontation may take a socially recognized form that even gains official legitimization, as in the case of the march, or mass public protest; it may take a secretly acceptable form, as in the negotiations forced by kidnappers, or it may assume a totally proscribed form, as in the case of bank robberies. These forms depend on constant repetition and a growing pattern of formalized procedures and rites, because they have not had an institutional framework to support them. As repression is pushed to the furthest degree, they may unleash a crescendo of violence that is directly proportional to the degree of conflict between the "establishment" and the "opposition." Social pressure is used to satisfy aspirations that could formerly be met within the rules of the political game and by existing institutional mechanisms. Ultimately, the political gesture becomes indistinguishable from the criminal. Bank robberies depend on their cumulative effect to emphasize to public opinion continuing aggression against the system.

Breaking down the forms of confrontation we find the following (see table 2, p. 46):

1) *Protest:* This appears in the political system when normal mechanisms for functional cooperation in society as a whole are eliminated. It exerts pressure by threatening to destroy the overall presumptions of agreement upon which the division of labor within the community at its various levels is based. This withdrawal of cooperation can take the form of (a) the interruption of certain roles in the mechanisms necessary to the functioning of the political subsystem as a whole, such as opposition in Parliament or breakdown of the electoral process; or (b) interference in the institutional procedures needed for the functioning of the political system. Protest action always embodies an infraction of the rules, of either the time or the place where protest is normally made manifest. So, for example, it may involve mass action apart from the election process or it may be carried on outside the framework of the legislature.[10] Such manifestations of dissent consist of marches or public rallies which translate originally "clandestine" protest into a genuine social plebiscite.

Outside the purely political field, protest may be expressed simply as the alteration of normal rules of social cooperation but not to the extent of interruption of the functioning of the society. It may take the form of picketing or of the sit-in. The sit-in is particularly preva-

Table 2
Typology of confrontation

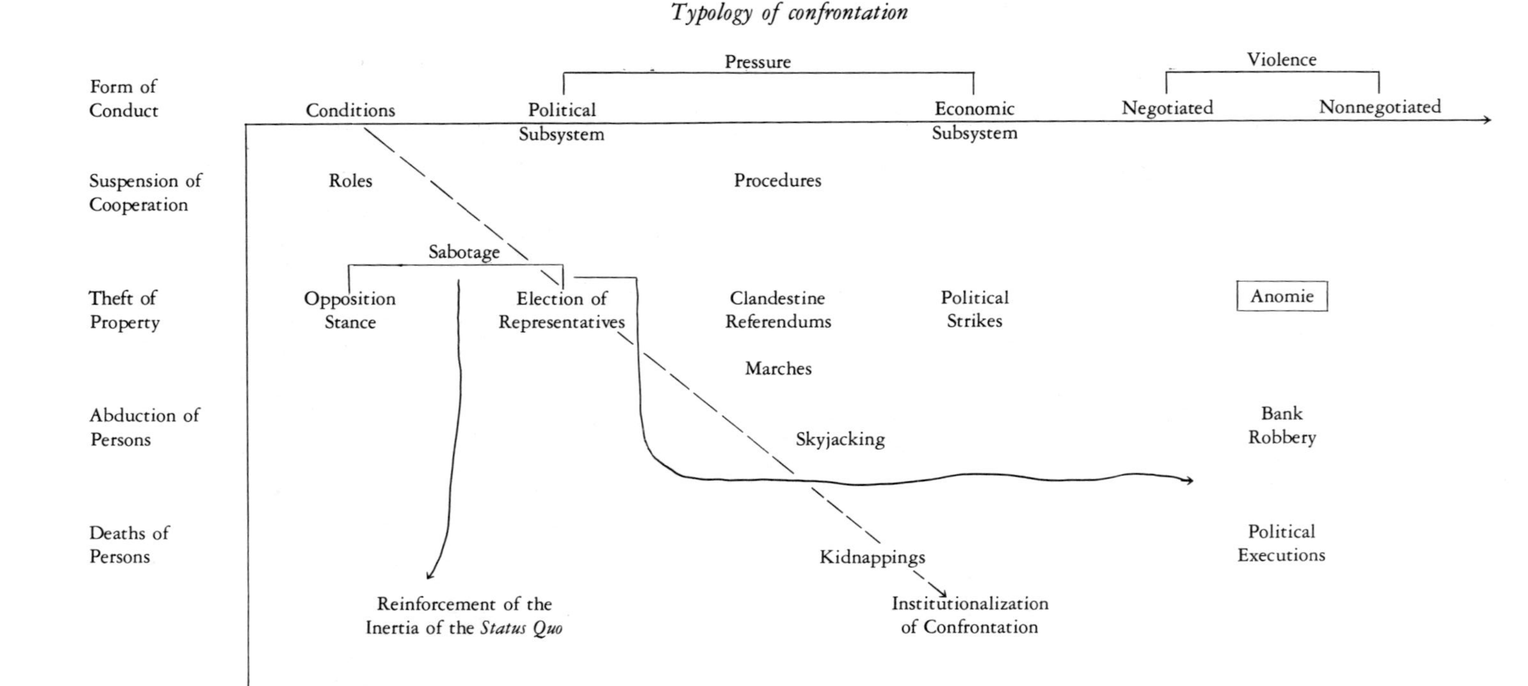

lent at the universities where normal expectations regarding disciplinary cooperation are disregarded. Without interrupting the operations of the institution, protest takes the form of occupying classrooms beyond the normal classroom hours for endless discussions.

2) *The political strike:* This is the abandonment, for reasons beyond the purely economic, of the cooperation which forms the basis of labor relations. It is the final resort when a community seeks to throw its collective weight against the regime's naked social oppression. But the political strike is a "limited" instrument; it avoids a final violent confrontation.[41] This type of protest has recently been illustrated in Argentina. In the limited strikes of Córdoba in 1970 the strikers went beyond strictly professional demands to take a political position. But by keeping their action localized and disciplined, they avoided a general strike, which could have released uncontrollable revolutionary forces.

3) *The limited or conditional use of violence* may occur in order to extract certain decisions or gestures from the power center. In general this method of confrontation is represented by political kidnappings. Its goal is propaganda by means of the media to make public opinion aware of the diffusion and the strength of social dissent. The ransom asked may be the liberation of antagonists of the system, but an additional symbolic level exists in that the size of the ransom is correlated to the negative or positive importance of the forces or the nations represented by the victim.

4) *The direct utilization of violence* may take the form of property damage or robbery. This form of confrontation seeks to emphasize an intention that goes beyond the mere content of the action. Each instance further unifies the symbolic act with the notion of permanent conflict with the regime. By ritual repetition the actors hope to impart a significance beyond mere criminality to their particular exploit. Thus, the phenomenon of continuous armed attacks on banks in certain Brazilian cities progressively created a clear profile of political opposition while at the same time providing the material means of confrontation with the establishment.

5) *Final recourse to violence.* This involves actions in the name of a so-called revolutionary justice which differ from those of generalized internal conflict or civil war. An example is the summary execution— despite a simulated judicial procedure—of former President Aram

buru of Argentina after his kidnapping in 1970. Ostensibly he was killed for abuse of power against the people while in office. Such an act is distinct from a normal kidnapping for ransom. Over and above the sense of reprisal and its dramatic effect, the execution shows symbolic evidence of dissent as a result of calculated logic in which such an action would be only one aspect of the general context of conflict. Acts of confrontation stop at the crucial point of change in the balance of strength between the "status quo" and the opposition; to go beyond would mean civil war. Terminal violence seeks to demonstrate points of no return to link the present situation with the past to intensify the target of a common stand against the regime.

The degree of confrontation

It is possible to relate, one to another, the different points in the scale of dissent leading to the full institutionalization of violence. It is also possible to detect in the acceleration and "standardization" of these acts of protest a demonstration effect linked to bank robbery and especially to skyjacking. A certain kind of institutional model seems to be emerging, especially in kidnapping: the premise of negotiation seems finally established. In Brazil, for example, everyone exchanged in this process of institutionalized struggle is banished from the country. Certain conventions of style are fixed, such as the credibility of messages and the value of the ransom. These conventions are not, however, nonnegotiable; they stem essentially from the practical level of discretionary decision which characterizes the power-elite regimes. The institutional model of political hijacking of planes, for example, is in process of change. Governments now seem more willing to risk intercepting the hijackers by exploiting opportunities at refueling points or at points of crew change.

The difficulties of escalation in the symbolic use of violence are clear. The actors in the confrontation are always held in check. On the one hand, their own norms require them to refrain from murder or generalized aggression against the community. On the other hand, they need to create a strong enough case to assure them of publicity so that the public can relate each individual action to a readily recognizable model of confrontation used by a specifically identifiable group. The necessarily rare and limited character of these gestures requires that the actors give priority to establishing a clear chain of relationships between different kidnappings so that they may be seen by the public as episodes in the same escalation.

The model of confrontation in the bipartisan system

The first level of confrontation is a deviation from normal behavior in the formal political arena that aims at blocking the activity or the role of the opposition within the mechanism of the legislative assembly. This implies a breakdown of legislative function; it can even be seen as a threat of self-dissolution on the part of the faction antagonistic to the government, which perceives that the government has reduced its decision-making role to a marginal level or has actually destroyed it.

In power-elite politics of a bipartisan sort, the parties are rigidly divided between the establishment and the opposition. The system is no longer dictated by a real representational principle; that is to say, the principle by which political bodies become the mediators within classes or among social groups in order to achieve ultimately a "general will" of all citizens. Within the framework of a rationalized and a programmatic view of development, the whole function of decision-making is transferred to those who are at the summit of power in the executive. The legislature, however, is maintained in a residual form to permit social recognition of this function.[42] In such an arrangement the effective role of the government party disappears, while the opposition carries out a limited function as a ratifying agent. If, however, the opposition refuses to ratify a decision, all semblance of national solidarity may be destroyed.[43] Instead of displaying the heterogeneity typical of representative bodies, this system indicates, at one and the same time, how much acceptance of or resistance to the supreme authority exists.

The bipartisan power-elite regime has nothing in common with models in which the political subsystem is the indispensable mediating mechanism between the social and economic subsystems.[44] In Brazil political parties such as ARENA (National Renovative Alliance) or the MDB (the Brazilian Democratic Movement) cannot be expected to play the same roles as they would if they had a real representative function. The task of the opposition party is not to enter into substantive debate and to participate in the formulation of laws, or indeed, even to aspire to direct negotiating power regarding the content of a decision. Its very limited role is to preserve, by its presence or by the threat of self-dissolution, separation between the political subsystem and the other subsystems of the society. The opposition plays exclusively a confrontational role, while simultaneously retaining the function of a "standby threat" (which is, in fact, its real role). In the power elite system the exercise of power does not depend on representation but on the capacity of the regime to mobilize the masses behind a rational and fully predetermined national development plan. The party system is confined to two well-defined roles— for the party in power, to support the decisions of the executive and for the opposition, to influence legislation by means of the threat of final self-dissolution if its voice is ignored.

It would be easy to argue that in power-elite regimes the point at which a prudent and rationalized resumption of the popular consultation takes place would be the point at which confrontation becomes rampant. The risk of holding elections derives from the power of the democratic tradition established during the populist era. Objectively, in Brazil limited free elections would have allowed the opposition party to obtain an appreciable number of seats in the national assembly, particularly in the cities with a population of more than 100,000, if the electoral system maintained intact simple majority-minority rules.

It must also be stressed that no *formal* measures exist in the power elite system to prevent the theoretical possibility of an opposition majority, however little effect this might have on the decision-making process. But the first elections held after 1964 proved that the opposition strategy was still to make use of the ballot an act of open dissent. But this negative gesture was blunted by the contradictory influences of the relations between status and class to be found in a developing society. The Brazilian election of 1966 proved that the possibility open to the opposition of obtaining increased electoral representation was greatly decreased because the opposition felt that it was necessary to make of the electoral consultation a manifestation of confrontation.

50

But to do so effectively required mobilization of the disciplined ranks of the labor unions. This would have produced in the Assembly a radical group strongly opposed to the regime.[45] Such a group would have been the dissident voice of a faction that has opted for a position effectively outside the new system. The final result had to be a drift toward violence; the real limits of the strategy of "negative dissent" should be examined in this context.

A strategy of negative dissent also exists. Staying away from the polls may indicate either an essentially ambiguous attitude toward the regime, opposition or inertia in the face of the *status quo.* Positive confrontation, expressed by massive voting, is therefore the usual course, especially in normal working-class centers, which are susceptible to intense union influence despite the ban on open organization after 1964. Of course, at the specific command of the union leader, dissent could take a symbolic form. Ballots would not be left blank, rather they would be destroyed or spoiled, or have opposition slogans written on them, thus changing electoral consultation into a secret referendum against the establishment.

It might therefore be assumed that, if the number of nullified or blank ballots corresponded closely to the number of radical votes, no significant rise in opposition activity had taken place. A large vote for candidates most strongly opposed to the establishment would confirm two levels of electoral dissent, one of those who continued to vote, the other of those who normally remained silent by not voting and who were thus marginal to political activity. If those candidates most opposed to the regime secured a large number of votes, this would constitute virtually a delegated representation of those who had voluntarily indicated their opposition by silence. However, examination of the 1966 Brazilian election returns indicates that, contrary to what might be supposed: (a) the areas in which the workers' vote predominates show a high level of possible voters but a small number of blank or nullified ballots, (b) workers tended to vote for those candidates supported by the mass media, as is characteristic of a low level of electoral mobilization and (c) radical candidates had a mediocre showing which indicated no reinforcement of opposition from a mass of nullified votes. The electoral results point to no real evidence that might allow us to establish gradations between radicals of the left who still vote and those who have gone beyond the limits of the normal institutional framework by destroying ballots or leaving them blank.

These results permit analysis of the extreme limitations imposed on mobilization of the proletarian vote as a manifestation of confrontation [46] in countries such as Brazil. While the influence of the power-elite regimes should not be underestimated in their ability to reduce the role of the trade unions and to place extreme limits upon the unions' capability to direct their membership in its electoral choices, the importance of this influence should not be exaggerated in the 1966 elections. But the essential reason the labor vote did not express its opposition through nullification lies in the deep attachment the worker has to the act of voting, which he sees as an important sign of social status.

The Brazilian proletariat has not yet attained that political stage in which it is prepared to carry out an act of personal privation—annulment of the vote—for the right to vote represents virtually the only contact the worker has with the political process. For the working class, destroying the ballot is neither a form of political communication nor even a sign of resistance.[47] It is a permanent severing of the special relationship in which political activity assumes a role as a bargaining instrument.

Under conditions of repression, the ability to exercise the franchise gains even greater significance for the working class; it symbolically expresses integration into international society. Radical protest in the form of the vote becomes blocked by the vote's metaphysical significance and the implied gesture of "social destruction" contained in the failure to exercise it. The breakdown of the class structure, combined with the frustrated efforts of the trade-union leaders to direct workers toward political confrontation, essentially reduced the proletariat in 1966 to a simple mass electorate. The first elections under the power-elite regime indicated a regression in working-class political action, since the workers allowed themselves to be influenced by the mass media and, in consequence, reinforced candidates who were not in the best interest of the workers. Lacking the necessary catalyst, the electoral act never became a mass movement of confrontation. After 1966, criticism became limited to the intelligentsia which, in turn, was never able to create a mechanism capable of transferring its activities to other social groups.

52

Dissent remained at a superficial level, mobilized by the weakest of links, the mass media.[48] Because of the lack of message in the media, dissent remained diffuse and unpolarized. The engaging and entertaining nature of the media masked its real victory over the electorate. The biggest winners in the election were those who were able to gain from the greatest exposure through their possession and use of television and the press.

The role of the mass media and the low level of mobilization in the electoral contest are simply a further result of the bipartisan nature of the power-elite system. The unrepresentative framework created by government neither produced common denominators nor integrated the different political and social groups that had grown up during the period of spontaneous development. The strictly "government party-opposition party" constitution avoided integration by recognizing superstructural mechanisms exclusively and by making the temporary composition of these mechanisms and the circumstances of their creation the central core of the new model. The votes gained by a candidate ultimately depended on his exposure in the mass media. Both voters and candidates were joined, then, by a new form of power—the party authorities, acting much of the time in the role of censors.

The lack of sociological dimension in the vote reflected the system's lack of representation. The dystrophic development model that distinguished "rationally" between the various social sectors given access to the privileges of development produced a political structure that rested on nonrepresentation and noncommunication of government with the body politic. The forced bipartisanship did little to reflect the social cleavages born of development. Rigid regulation of party and parliamentary life, to which was added the very reduced function of the legislature, confined political activity to the internal dynamic of the superstructure and to the power struggle within the government and the central directorate of the parties. If to this is added the strong influence of the mass media and their greater emphasis on form than on content, the unlikelihood of real parliamentary dissent becomes clear. With no specific sociological base, it could only act as a pseudoopposition based on false alliances and dealing with irrelevant problems.

Short-circuiting the representational system by means of the march

In any enumeration of the forms of confrontation, another departure from conventional institutionalization of political activity must be analyzed. Marches of large collective gatherings are, in effect, a kind of "wild" plebiscite. In the march, confrontation gives visible evidence of opinion *outside* the electoral setting. This form of mass mobilization has within it its own dynamic; by seriously disturbing public order it can push any political system to the limits of its absorptive capacity.

It is significant that the fully institutionalized mechanisms of mass marches [49] found in the present (1970) European and American [50] regimes have also arisen in the underdeveloped countries at a critical stage of the spontaneous-change phase. Marches display a power that is beyond the system from the very outset. In effect, this manifestation of opinion drawn from the "heart of the people" makes it necessary to give to political decisions an appearance of response to the popular will. In view of the critical political and economic conditions at the beginning of the sixties, mass marches or meetings were brought into being by an irreversible imperative. However, contrary to the intention of their European counterparts, the marches in Brazil were meant to create a state of political mobilisation which would have prevented any return to the *status quo ante.* Such was the power of making the masses "visible" that it became the principal strategy of the protest movement. It seemed, by its hidden implications, to make possible a change in power relationships.

Meta-marches

The collapse of the populist political system in Brazil in 1964 was produced by a contradictory succession of mass gatherings which brought into question the entire relationship of power within the country. At the beginning, the government associated the popular case for abandoning the democratic system with a model of a trade-union republic; this demand was stimulated by the great meeting of

54

ratification and solidarity in support of the populist platform of 13 March 1964, which brought together some two hundred thousand people in Rio de Janeiro.

Some days later a countermanifestation took place, provoked by a deep emotional reaction to the threat to conventional forms of popular consultation. The counterdemonstration was clearly the work of those social strata directly threatened by any possible trade-union state. In particular this meant the diverse establishment groups and especially the urban middle class.[51] In the Brazilian context, however, the countermarch not only manifested a demand for the *status quo,* but at the same time, it was also a confrontation aimed at questioning the legitimacy of a government that sought to break down the entire institutional framework of the society. But it should be emphasized that both factions required some kind of objective legitimacy before introducing extreme measures for change in the regime. None of the groups involved in the counterdemonstration dared take the usual steps leading to a *coup d'etat,* or to revolutionary action, without a prior commitment of support from the popular majority. In this way the marches became a public-opinion poll, although a highly risky one, since this type of action has many unexpected and uncontrollable aspects.

The institutional absorption of the march

For all practical purposes, the marches precipitated a government crisis. The capacity to withstand such a demonstration might be seen as a great test of the solidity of a technocratic system. If the march can be "absorbed" by the system, the reward is a defusing of tensions at a moment of peak confrontation. The march itself became a manifestation of genuine community which channeled dissent into a form of intense, almost choreographic expression—an innovative act of civic sublimation. On those limited occasions when marches did take place, they clearly revealed the fragility of the legitimacy sought by the system. This can be seen, for example, in the series of marches in the former State of Guanabara between April and June 1968, which culminated in the March of the Hundred Thousand. Participants in this last enormous manifestation seemed, however, unconscious of its inherent capacity for extended action. Although tolerated by the regime, the march was supervised by a vast deployment of security forces. Among the marchers pressed against the police barriers were supporters of great social prestige whose very presence provoked respect. It was not surprising that members of the clergy occupied important places in the march, walking at the head and protecting its flanks.

The march permitted, within the moveable, but restricted, limits of confrontation permitted by the regime a remarkable degree of participation in the expression of dissent. In the brief moment in which it took form and flourished, the march found its deepest meaning and its greatest potential as a vehicle for the expression of dissent.

The march of the Hundred Thousand proved that a number of the catchwords or "mottos" used by the protest groups could be reduced to two or three basic catch phrases which were transformed during the march into sonorous, modulated sounds, which unexpectedly found half-audible echo among the on-lookers. The march, which, by its very rhythm, liberated the energies of protest so long repressed, took on a progressively greater cohesion. It became not the melancholy and disciplined lines of European marches but an elegantly choreographed gigantic ballet. It was as though the strength of the march was expressed in a final crescendo, the coordinated rhythm of which profoundly articulated the entire meaning of confrontation and exhausted it.

4 The resort to violence

Political strikes

Among the forms of confrontation, political strikes are one of the most delicate instruments. They require a high potential level of dissent and presume the presence of actors who do not have a majority voice yet in political institutions and pressure groups. They are subject to two inevitable limitations; on the one hand, it is difficult for the proletariat to go beyond their economic dissatisfaction in order to present, in a common front, their political opposition to the regime. On the other, strikes are hard to control once they break out and more than any other activity they force the government to step up its response and thus to reduce the degree of tolerance in the system. The nature of the conflict makes more urgent the declaration of a state of crisis, which is the last step before civil war.

It is understandable why the economic stability and the general atmosphere of development created by military-technocratic systems make it extremely difficult—particularly in Brazil—to use a mode of confrontation which is based on dissent existing in the salaried groups and even more so among the working class controlled by trade unions. Hence the difficulty the intelligentsia has had—as we will see later—in carrying their political activism beyond the students, the church, and certain well-defined intellectual groups. It is difficult for the proletariat, barring an initiative from the regime itself, to succeed in bringing into the rank and file any wide representation of these special groups. Latin America, and especially Brazil, cannot count, in the face of the power-elite regimes, on the integration of student groups and intellectuals with the proletariat. The events of May 1968 in Paris represent a situation which is *sui generis;* in all probability it is applicable only to a European framework and typical only of societies which have gained maturity and are on the road to abundance.

The lack of proletarian response shown to the street demonstrations in that year explains even more clearly the difficulty of mobilizing for a strike which has been transformed, in both its challenge and its risks, into political action. Even if a strike will not create such tension as might inspire military intervention, it will be difficult to motivate the salaried class toward any purely political action in the context of an atmosphere of economic expansion. This is especially true when the government maintains a strategic image of satisfying the masses.

An important paradox must be raised in the case of the developing countries that succeed in avoiding the impact of what the Almond/Pye scheme calls the "crisis of participation" in the process of change.[1] Because underdeveloped countries are not sufficiently mature, the political situation does not always create an awakening of consciousness or an effort toward mobilization.[2] Increased demand for participation, for example, may be paid off by a system of special allocations or by the granting of direct economic privileges within the development process; one may view it as a kind of ransom for aspirations to political power. As the first nodules of prosperity appear in these countries, a conservative, "establishment" attitude may develop in the salaried sector of the economy, which is closely tied to the most advanced levels of development and to those enterprises most closely connected with modernization. We have already mentioned that the proletariat regards the right to vote as a sign of social status. This tends to produce a deliberate indifference to politics, unlike the interest the proletariat have in gaining economic benefits and selective redistribution of wealth.[3] This happens in renewed programs of rationalized development, as in Brazil, where the government has adopted a strategy of controlled and preferential action for the redistribution of the national income.

At the present time in Latin America, examples of political strikes are mostly found in Argentina (for instance, the repeated actions in Córdoba in 1969). Work stoppage, not only in the transformation sectors, but also in certain public services, was clearly occasioned by more than a pure wage problem. But to be successful, these actions required strong support from the oldest and most deeply rooted trade-union movement on the continent, the Perónist General Confederation of Labor, which had one of its strongest bases in Córdoba.

These strikes in the Argentine, which took place at the edge of the pampas, turned ultimately toward isolated and intransigent episodes of confrontation which wasted the virtually unique opportunity for a decisive outbreak which the repressed opposition to Perónism might have supported. The violence accompanying the strikes not only provoked repression, but led in the end to a Pyrrhic victory. The eruption of violence left no other option than a continuous radicalization of the political process, which inevitably gave the *status quo* a tactical advantage. The circumstances in which this unprecedented strike developed are practically a model. There was an almost symmetrical division between government and the opposition, between the establishment-military alliance on one side and the salaried sector of Latin America's most disciplined trade-union structure on the other.

It was a step backward in the program of decompression that followed the events of Córdoba. In fact, it killed the cautious but determined first venture in attempting to open the system referred to as Ongania's *participacionismo*.

The gesture of violent confrontation: bank robberies

Today in situations of rationalized development in Latin America, dissent goes beyond the simple breakup of the models of social action and makes systematic the use of violence by an exasperated minority.[4] This study cannot undertake to analyze those confrontations which climax in an open struggle or even such underground operations as the urban guerrilla movement. These phenomena deserve exhaustive analysis, according to the specific circumstances of the collapse of spontaneous growth, and the stratification and mobilization in each country. We will concentrate rather on the use of violence as the repeated sign of social dissent. On the one hand, violent action does clear criminal damage to others, but gradually its meaning as part of the confrontation becomes clear only when the violence spreads more widely. What is important to emphasize is the clear purpose attached to continued, uninterrupted, and unappeasable violence. Through successive reiteration, the gesture of antagonism is contained within an act of common criminality.[5] It emphasizes the feeling of specific harassment by which, in the developing countries, the urgan guerrilla movement can be contrasted with classic rural forms. The "unappeasable" use of violence has brought to the metropolitan regions of these countries a new sense of exasperation.

The exact point at which repeated violence is regarded as normal activity, aimed at the nerve centers of society, cannot yet be verified. This does not mean simply the realization of its existence by the media and by public opinion. From the beginning, in Brazil, complete exclusion of the dissenters from the mass media destroyed any possibility of an "effective" climax. The curtain of silence around the bank robberies killed in embryo the mobilizing possibilities inherent in the use of crime. Publicity is the principal objective of this ulterior form of confrontation, just as it is the real payoff for the risk assumed by the demand for ransom in political kidnappings. Confrontation turns at that point from a formula of unappeasable violence into one of negotiated and institutionalized violence.

The confrontation sought in bank robberies succeeds only through broadening the gesture by repeated acts. Its effect is obviously weakened if the cumulative effect never becomes known, for then the marginal aspect, its criminal profile, will be emphasized, while the origins of its motivation in social dissent will be concealed. Attacking banks has become a standard activity, and although these acts may not come to the attention of the public, the actors always hope to benefit from the robbery in order to obtain the ways and means of sustaining the threat.

Bank robberies must become frequently repeated, ritual gestures if they are to leave the impress of a political goal. At the same time, the importance to the dissidents of inserting political significance into certain common crimes must be emphasized in the global perspective of institutionalized confrontation. The action becomes a private language, an indispensable means of expressing radical protest in which logistical and monetary gain is high. Constant harassment turns into the perfect mechanism to force a decisive test of strength, a final challenge to the establishment's solidarity. In effect, crime, even if motivated by political antagonism becomes the ideal way to draw the "excessive response," a blind thrashing about by those in authority. These violent exchanges lead to the establishment of a general balance of forces that might, in turn, lead to the possibility of reaching a "negotiated" level of violence, with pre-determined steps of escalation and escalation-control.

Skyjacking

In relation to bank robbery, skyjacking is a modified form of recourse to violence. It is extremely risky, but its potential "demonstration effect" is very great.

Acts of skyjacking in Latin America differ from the aerial piracy designed to extract ransom that is one criminal activity in today's affluent society. The bargaining aspect moves between a threat of imminent catastrophe and the return of control over the plane. But within these limits violence is minimized as an effective instrument. There is negotiation, but it is a "lightning negotiation," with no induced or threatened acts on the part of the establishment. Unlike the bank holdup, which beyond its intrinsic symbolism has immediate monetary advantages, the objective of skyjacking is a concentrated and dramatic gesture of strength instantly accomplished in the air. It relies on the dramatic effect of the action to raise the official curtain of silence. The gesture speaks so loudly that the perpetrators rarely give any further explanation for the act. On those rare occasions when official statements say more than simply that the incident occurred, they no longer take the form of memoranda or long explanations, as was the case of the communiqués relating to the early kidnappings. Little by little, as skyjacking has become the most widely used form of a negotiated violence in Latin America, as a general rule the statement by the perpetrators will simply refer to the celebration of a revolutionary anniversary, seeking a tie to significant facts in the perspective of confrontation in the entire Latin American continent.

Among the twenty-three skyjackings which took place between February 1969 and October 1972 in Latin America, in only one case did the skyjacking cease to be an end in itself. Of all the incidents which took place in Brazil, that of 1 July 1970 was the first in which the skyjackers demanded not only a change in routing, but the liberation of a specific number of political prisoners as well. In addition they demanded that the exchange be guaranteed by the forced embarkation on the plane of individuals who had the clearest symbolic prestige, two of the four Brazilian cardinals. This was the first time negotiations were broken off and the government, at great risk, did not give in; the plane was on the ground and the skyjackers were eventually captured. Except for this case, however, skyjacking appears to be a half-way point between the hold-up and kidnapping (which employs violence in an instrumental and accessory fashion). In terms of confrontation, skyjacking represents an intrasigent gesture of confrontation. It is self-sufficient, designed for its publicity effect. Propaganda value is maximized, while logistical or monetary gains are practically nil.

The only positive result of skyjacking, beyond its demonstration effect, is to protect revolutionaries from punishment under the anti-subversion laws and from the penalties of perpetual banishment or removal from the community. It might be argued, however, that a secondary effect of skyjacking is that the skyjackers obtain a self-imposed exile. However, recent evidence leads to the hypothesis that some are merely repeating the act and thus exile and asylum represent only one stop on a continuous circuit.

One may question whether the benefits of the operation are worth the enormous risks entailed for both the perpetrators and everyone else. Paradoxically, it is the size of the risk that has favored the "institutionalization" of subsequent procedure. The unimaginable cost of a breakdown in negotiations forces a predisposition to negotiate. A climate of concession is imposed. The clearly international impact of the gesture, as well as the volume of risk capital at stake (which ranges from the amount lost simply by deviation of the aircraft from its normal itinerary to the possible destruction of the plane), are only a part of these costs.

It is not surprising, consequently, that aerial piracy produces an almost automatic reaction. The crew does not ordinarily resist, and there is even cooperation on the part of the ground crew in replenishing stores when the new journey requires it. The absence of any effective means of preventing skyjacking allows this form of violence to become a *routinized* form of confrontation. In effect, everything proceeds as though this form of protest had been integrated into the social framework—a protest whose technological content makes society, paradoxically, virtually defenseless against it. Because of all the logistical considerations, the mechanisms of social coercion and response tend to be paralyzed. The cabin of a jet becomes the contemporary—and objectively inviolable—version of the medieval sanctuary.

Kidnappings

Kidnappings are the most institutionalized form of of radical political confrontation for those who accept that they are a minority in relation to the establishment.[6] This recognition signifies a maturing of the opposition in two senses: it recognizes the real relationship between the forces involved and it prepares for a complex and long-drawn-out effort. The question, however, is not merely one of recognizing the special character that gestures such as kidnapping represent in the scale of confrontation. They are not transient and spontaneous expressions of dissent but represent the use of violence as an instrument of bargaining and of calculated pressure in the framework of long-range opposition to the system. Kidnappings introduce into confrontation certain elements of game theory.[7] The costs and benefits of these extreme actions must be figured within the context of a maximum challenge to society. They define the sudden movements of escalation or retreat that are found in fully articulated confrontation. To analyze kidnapping as an instrument of negotiated violence, one must investigate the exchange itself and the procedure by which this form of bargaining has gained an institutionalized content as a specific instrument of confrontation.

The content of the exchange
and the limits of negotiation

In the majority of cases, one may presume that kidnapping will lead to imprisonment of the kidnappers; it may also lead to violence and often death for members of the security forces. In general the victims are important foreigners, which assures maximum international repercussions. The victims are usually representatives of countries or systems thought to be directly associated with the home regime either because of their economic policies or because of their preferences in foreign policy.

So far as the cost evaluation is concerned, Argentina provides a classic case of inadequate return. The victim was a diplomat of lower rank from Paraguay. When the authorities formally refused to cooperate or even respond to the kidnappers' demands, the kidnappers did not execute the hostage, as they had, under identical circumstances, the German ambassador in Guatemala. Instead they set the victim at liberty. In this case, quite apparently, there was too great a disproportion between the risk assumed and the potential gain. The final bargaining remained, so to speak, below the cost price and determined the captors gesture of magnanimity. Official lack of interest in a final confrontation emphasized the hostage's low "price"; he was, in fact, abandoned to his fate.

Generally, however, the victim's home government takes directly the opposite approach. It becomes a principal in the resolution of the situation, forcing, by direct intervention, the government immediately concerned in the affair to bring negotiation to a successful conclusion. Kidnapping immediately and automatically initiates an international response. In Brazil, total concern for the victim's physical well-being is clearly why the regime is inclined to accept bargaining as a fundamental condition. Argentina is still undecided, since no kidnapping of a very high-ranking foreign hostage has yet occurred. Large firms, particularly the multinational corporations, and not ambassadors, have been the goal, and businessmen are victims of low visibility. Two kidnappings—those of the local president of Fiat, Oberdan Sallustro (who was finally executed in April 1972) and directors of petroleum and cold storage companies (who were ransomed after direct and secret negotiations—illustrate the difficulty of establishing a bargaining situation outside a framework directly related to the prestige factors of national sovereignty.

In Argentina kidnapping as mere political harassment ended for all practical purposes in January 1973, when forces of the classic populist left transformed kidnapping into an instrument of semicivil war. For the next seven months kidnappings took place virtually every seventy-two hours. They assumed practically the same connotation as bank robberies in that, for the most part, monetary ransom became the essential point of the operation.

An important factor in the institutionalization of kidnapping is the degree of solidarity of the system that is being challenged. This was illustrated when West Germany's Ambassador Von Spreti was kidnapped in Guatemala. In this case external pressures played a full role; the government of the Federal Republic joined with the Pope and most representative organizations of the international intelligentsia to intervene. But these groups ran head on into the absolute refusal of the government of Guatemala to engage in any negotiation. This grim attitude arose in part from Guatemala's difficulty in regulating its own internal conflicts and from the potential dangers involved in making concessions. The dramatic resolution of the case, Ambassador Von Spreti's execution, pointed up very clearly the sociopolitical support that is required for flexible solutions in these negotiations and the necessity for basic solidarity of the regime which any ostensible deviation from the conventional code of international order requires.

A further illustration of this is to be found in Uruguay, where in later 1968 the government steadfastly refused to negotiate in the face of several kidnappings of people important in the financial world. The uniqueness of the cases rests in the violence of the nature of the counterresponse the kidnappers generally made to the Pacheco Areco government's intractability.[8] One reason the Uruguayan kidnappings were atypical may have been that the contestants had as yet not determined the exact degree of support they would elicit from the community.

At the time Uruguay was neither in the process of development, nor was it trying a new technocratic and authoritarian approach to settle an impending crisis. It was, rather, a clear example of economic regression, in which a cumulative decline in the expansion of the gross national product was taking place in a country where an extremely high percentage of the population are in the tertiary sector of economy—their income is regulated by a system of statutory distribution of revenue. Because of the already low level of national income, it was very difficult to get a great deal of collective support for a serious mobilization of the economy. Unlike other Latin American countries which have experienced a renaissance of development, dissenting groups in Uruguay may achieve some degree of solidarity with certain social classes. They benefit, if not from mutual support, at least from a diffuse climate of consent which has been totally lacking in opposition group action in Brazil and Argentina.

The Uruguayan case underlines an ambiguity in the profile of the Tupamaros. Through their potential for disturbance, their calculated violence, and their effort to dramatize confrontation, they have created a form of protest which introduces, even into an action supporting the establishment, a means of overthrowing it. Such a condition creates great potential for breaking down the solidarity of the *status quo,* and the Tupamaros therefore hesitate before taking decisive actions, such as carrying out the threat of kidnapping, which might lose them tacit popular approval. They tend to restrain their action in order not to alienate those social groups now united by a diffuse sentiment opposing the regime. Consequently, a positive aspect may be seen in their possible use of violence as an answer to the government's refusal to negotiate. They are groping for a response which will look to the public like continuous escalation rather than merely action and immediate reaction. In these circumstances, confrontations are not merely threats and responses; they are continued indefinite adjournments of discussion, the content of which, over time, changes substantially. It is as though kidnappings were only a preliminary action on which later confrontation will be built; they are aimed at a progressive encouragement of latent discontent.

In this specific dynamic, then, the Uruguayan kidnappings may be seen as strong, but indefinite and equivocal, signs of tension. Kidnappings are one of many actions which have a potential capacity to create resentment against the *status quo.* After the first response, there is always a groping, after many false starts, in directions which may turn either to execution or to release of the victim, as a result of a *retrospective* evaluation of what has really been put to the test by the kidnapping. Governmental obstinacy returns the ultimate decision each time to those engaged in the confrontation; it forces them to redefine their intentions. Hence, the moment of the abduction is only the beginning of the dialectic. It may end in the death of the hostage or, after a long period of captivity, in his liberation. Generally, the model followed is that of an initial suspension of the sentence of execution in order to give the kidnappers the opportunity of appearing to be magnanimous, even in the face of the government's rigid attitude of non-cooperation. This was true in the case of the Brazilian consul and of a member of the American Economic Cooperation Mission in Uruguay. Under these circumstances, the challenge reverts to mere skirmishing. The kidnappers wish to maintain their freedom of initiative until after they have gauged the degree to which their ac-

66

tion has created public support for their cause and helped to change their minority position in the country.

What are the real margins of negotiation open to governments challenged by kidnappings? Those in power may be subject to unexpected and weakening limitations; for example, the transfer of negotiations from the local scene to the international. This loss of initiative may be reduced in the degree to which it becomes possible to adopt, on the scene, an incontestably dominant position vis-a-vis potential dissident factions and groups who are at present part of the system.

A correlation must first be established between the political solidarity of the systems challenged and their predisposition to negotiate for hostages. That is to say, the demands of those engaged in confrontation will force those in power to confront their system of values and priorities, which are linked, of course, to the very existence of the established social order. Regime solidarity may be reflected in its skill at lowering the stakes and avoiding brutal alternatives. Particularly in those governments of an authoritarian character, the problem of respecting human life meets head-on questions of national prestige or the integrity of collective discipline. Even when the government decides to give to such values the same weight as they might have in a conventional democratic regime, one must not underestimate the cumulative effect that automatic negotiation may have on challenged authoritarian governments. This is particularly true of the most radical factions, which tend to reduce the concept of social order purely to a mechanism of collective subordination.

Gradation of objectives in kidnappings

From the kidnappers' point of view the goal of negotiation has two aspects. First, as the Brazilian case indicates, it is to send out, through the media, messages and proclamations which will lead the public to recognize how strong and widespread the opposition network is. There is also an exchange aspect—hostages will be freed in return for political prisoners. As part of its defensive mechanism the Brazilian establishment has tried to limit the benefits resulting from the liberation of political prisoners. The automatic "predisposition to negotiate" has been offset by the sentence of banishment applied to liberated prisoners. Their unilateral inclusion in the lists of those to be freed brings in its train a summary imposition of the new punishment imposed on all those released through negotiation, thus relegating the ransomed captive to a completely passive element in the whole operation.

In this type of exchange, the symbolic aspects must be emphasized. The kidnappers must sacrifice the personal interest of the political prisoner to his symbolic value. The first lists of those to be liberated seemed preoccupied with making clear to the public the variety of those social groups engaged in the opposition struggle. Rarely was a direct or personal connection played on, for fear that the family or friends might become the medium of exchange and thereby run the same risks. As for the abductors, they risked certain banishment.

The characteristics of these operations (for instance, their wide range of victims) leads us to believe that we are dealing with a small group, which has very little internal cohesion. Members are probably unconnected with traditional terrorist action or already highly structured and professionalized subversive organizations. This conclusion is further reinforced by the fact that one dominant social trait of such dissidents is their youth. Only a very few of the kidnappings could be described as the end of a *continuum* of confrontations in which a clear and intentional relationship existed between the kidnappers and those who benefited from their action.

Negotiation in the Guatemalan kidnapping, however, concealed a third dimension. The predominant objective was not gaining access to the media, as in the Brazilian and Argentinian cases. Not only did the kidnappers want prisoners exchanged for the hostages, they also demanded money. Clearly kidnapping was also to provide the logistical means with which to continue the confrontation, which would ultimately become open and generalized conflict. The virtual absence of a demand by the abductors for publicity in the "package" is understandable. In the limited territories of small nations (such as the Central American republics) foreign control of what media exist limits its utility in kidnappings.

The emerging institutionalization of kidnapping

In the drama of these tests of strength certain patterns of reaction grew up; kidnapping began to "institutionalize": The reactions occurred in the heat of the moment, but they simultaneously created a stimulus-response model of communication between the parties. The model was characterized from the first by its fully public aspect—there were no secret negotiations—and more particularly by the absence of mediators or arbitrators in the final transactions. Fundamentally a system was established in which the participants exchanged communications via newspapers, radio, or television. Not only did the mass media publish news of the kidnappings but it carried the kidnappers' message as well. This also permitted the publication of coded passwords established by the kidnappers which were to be used by government as proof that the measures required of it were being carried out, thus establishing a secret as well as a public dialogue between the negotiating parties.

In the Brazilian case, the very form of the government response clearly demonstrated the principle that it was prepared to use negotiation to establish conditions for liberation. In the Argentine case, the government's delays made it evident that it would, in fact, try to refuse to negotiate. The government claimed, for example, that it could not possibly meet the kidnappers' demands, either by denying the arrest of the prisoners or by claiming they were dead or had disappeared. There have not yet been enough incidents to know whether such dilatory tactics will prevent continued negotiation, or whether the abductors will consent to replace on the list of those to be liberated others with equal symbolic value. It should be emphasized that, in the dramatic case of a kidnapping which turned out badly—that of Ambassador Von Spreti—the government refused to negotiate because it claimed that the prisoners were either dead or had disappeared and that an excessive sum was required to effect the exchange. In fact, the ransom posed no problem, since the Bonn government, as a secondary participant, had offered to pay it on the spot.

It is important to reemphasize the significance of the process of exchange itself. The meaning attributed to each element of the negotiation must be studied, particularly in relation to the weight assigned, for example, to the number of hostages or to the values questioned in this test of strength. The publicity attached to the operation is in itself a message; public opinion is made aware of an active opposition capable of making those in authority listen. The negotiating messages allow an act of violence to be placed in an explicitly political context; not only do they clarify the opposition's political position, they also permit symbolic manipulation by establishing a relationship between the choice of victim and that of the prisoners to be liberated. An entirely new dimension of the exchanges emerges from the weights the kidnappers establish.

Kidnapping important foreigners is a way of symbolizing the revolutionary struggle of the exploited against the exploiters—whether they be countries or social classes. When the victims are the representatives of the great powers, particularly those playing a leading role in the local economy, their kidnapping produces the greatest impact, has an easily distinguishable symbolic meaning, and permits the stakes in negotiation to be raised. The value of the ransom is proportionate to the power of victims' country. The fact that the scale of ransom has not always been parallel to the power position of the foreign country suggests that an inverse plan may exist. It is possible that, as an object lesson, the abductors choose to "devalue" the country concerned in the eyes of public opinion. Instead of recognizing its power by demanding a large ransom, they show their low esteem by demanding only a small sum.

Such may have been the rationale the Brazilian abductors used in fixing the ransoms for the series of kidnappings begun in 1969. The first, that of US Ambassador Elbrick in August 1969, required the lowest ransom of all—the exchange of five prisoners. Fifteen or sixteen were asked for the consul-general of Japan in Rio de Janiero and fifty for the ambassador of the German Federal Republic, Honleben. It might even be hypothesized that the heavy ransom demanded for him was a result of the relatively minor presence of his country in Brazil as compared to Japan. In short, the hostage became a useful symbol of the value the dissenters attached to a particular country.

The dynamic of kidnapping

The effect of "entropy" in the rapid and easy institutionalization of kidnapping cannot be denied in view of the escalating nature of its symbolic language. Its effect is clearly reinforced by repetition, and the increase in the exchange rate progressively erodes the limits of governmental resistance when confronted by kidnapping. Governments view institutionalization of kidnapping as a means of establishing a point of no return in the negotiation and, consequently, as a way to measure the risk taken in case the predisposition to negotiate breaks down. One must realize how extremely sensitive governments are to the demonstration effect of these unprecedented techniques of confrontation. The tragic resolution of the Guatemalan case increased the necessity of prudence; it made clear both the danger of inflexible government response and the narrow range of negotiating capability possessed by the kidnappers.

When the Organization of American States discusses this particular problem, heavy emphasis is increasingly laid on reinforcing mechanisms for discouraging kidnapping and for limiting its consequences rather than on firmness in negotiation. It becomes indispensable to formalize the genuine state of urgency created by kidnapping and to obtain an international agreement that risks will not be taken, rather than agreement on an *a priori* refusal to negotiate with the kidnappers.

In terms of game theory, institutionalization gives an intrinsic tactical advantage to those engaged in confrontation. In general, a basic goal of a kidnapping is to present a demand and a manifesto as a preamble to the opening of negotiation and to any discussion of exchange. The desired publicity effect is a direct result. Discussions are then inaugurated with an irreversible tactical advantage for the kidnappers.

Adroitly exploited, this initial advantage favors long-term effective action against the regime because of its corrosive effect on authoritarian regimes which depend on an acute sense of hierarchy and on rigid social subordination. Emphasis on essential values and on respect for life and physical well-being are at the base of every "civilized" social system, according to the internationally recognized rules of the game. Adherence to these rules determines how open a regime is to the international system within which it operates. In view of the rigid codes of honor and prestige practiced by any corporate form of government, a political model such as the power elite finds itself especially badly placed to act in a manner compliant with the expectations of international society. The demands of a "universal conscience" constitute a special burden for this type of government. It places the regime at one and the same time in a position which contradicts the imperative of hierarchy, which tries to maintain its own social organization and yet respect universal human values. On the one hand, the government faces external demands for flexibility in negotiation and, on the other, it wishes to preserve its authority and symbolic prestige. Certainly in Brazil at least, a common pacifist tradition, indeed a national ethos of "friendliness," reinforces the institutionalization of negotiation. But its effect should not be overestimated; the massive social costs of these kidnappings may well lead to an intransigence that is much closer to the nature of the power elite regime.

The most recent series of kidnappings shows that their initial dynamic may have reached its limit; the gain may be doubtful, hence the terms of the negotiations are becoming less clear as the abductors seek to gain new advantages from their actions. The kidnapping of Swiss Ambassador Bucher in December 1970 in the former State of Guanabara revealed a change of attitude on the part of the Brazilian government. The regime increased its margin of risk by rejecting the first conditions of negotiation and by narrowing the forms of exchange. In this fourth Brazilian kidnapping, the abductors suddenly increased the number of prisoners to be exchanged from fifty to seventy. They made an all-out effort to assure that this new exchange ceiling would be met. In addition they raised the level of their expectations by introducing a new kind of demand. The two sides continued their search for a middle point at which the advantages held by the abductors would always be kept slightly below the point at which negotiations would break down entirely. The abductors could only keep negotiations going by renouncing all collateral effects of the exchange and by abandoning their initial gains, including the publication of manifestos. The government, however, consistently refused from the very beginning to accede to a demand by the kidnappers that would have had spectacular propaganda value, namely, giving the people free access to consumer goods and services to improve living conditions. Such, for example, was the demand for free travel for two days on suburban trains.

It is significant that of the original demands, the only one to be retained was the number of persons to be exchanged for the hostage.

The list of the political prisoners to be released was constantly being modified; only the number of prisoners to be liberated persisted, but on this the kidnappers stood fast. By accepting at the very beginning changes in the names, the government gained an advantage and the discussions began to develop in a fashion quite different from the preceding cases. This is evident from the complex transactions concerning the names presented in the first list. Moreover, this time the government made it clear to those prisoners involved that they had the choice between remaining in the country or participating in the exchange operation with all the subsequent penalties (i.e., banishment) attached to it. There was a simultaneous weakening in the initial bargaining power of the kidnappers, since they were no longer capable of imposing their conditions on the government unilaterally. It might be argued that the questionable results obtained, as the kidnappers' bargaining position weakened, may be explained by the Swiss hostage's comparative unimportance, and doubts the kidnappers had about how much risk the government would be disposed to accept.

In any event, kidnapping seemed to have lost its usefulness as a tool of confrontation. The fact that the kidnappers renounced any claim to control negotiations through the mass media and thus to utilize public opinion as a challenge to the government and as an element of confrontation, represents a significant departure from the initial tendency of such protest action. Only continuing concern on the part of the Brazilian government to preserve the lives of hostages tended to make possible the survival of kidnapping as an instrument of confrontation. A profound reformulation of the advantages of negotiated violence had to be made. No longer could each successive challenge multiply the amount of the ransom, henceforth it would be necessary to limit the objective. It is symptomatic that when a company manager who symbolized the large foreign industries in the Argentine was kidnapped in June 1971, the price for liberation was revision of wages, improvement of working conditions, and distribution to employees of clothing and woolen goods manufactured by this industry. These demands replaced all other forms of ransom, such as money or exchange of prisoners.

Terminal violence: the execution of General Aramburu

The ultimate in this type of confrontation is nonnegotiable terminal violence. An execution, taking the form of retributive justice, demonstrates dramatically to public opinion that the kidnappers consider their opposition to be permanent; they seek to relate their threat to a permanent situation of conflict and by doing so to regroup and mobize the forces of latent opposition in the system. Such was the case in 1970 when Argentinian Montoneros kidnapped former President Aramburu, who had been head of the government responsible for the fall of Juan Perón in 1955. It was clear in this instance (unparalled in Latin America) that there was only the appearance of negotiation. Impossible prices were asked for the freedom of this super-hostage, such as the liberation of political prisoners who were known to be dead. The act was designed to reinforce the impact of confrontation in the popular mind by juxtaposing it with news that these prisoners were dead. Until Aramburu's abduction, this had been a jealously guarded secret. The kidnappers also wanted to force the Onganía government to avow publicly the degree of anti-Perónist repression. Exceptional ransom was demanded initially on the principle of so-called revolutionary justice. But the very confession by the regime that the prisoners had been executed assured the former president's death. No exchange alternatives were offered, despite the regime's broadly demonstrated predisposition to negotiate. The abductors did seek to create an atmosphere of counterlegitimacy by preceding the execution with a kind of mock tribunal and they took the life of the former president only after listening to the accused. But nothing the Argentine government could have done would have avoided the expiation of the alleged crime of 1955.

The "legal" trial and condemnation of Aramburu was designed to pose a revolutionary legitimacy against governmental legitimacy. The whole affair had a twofold objective. In the first place it was an attempt to show that despite the passage of fifteen years and the ambiguous presidencies of Frondizi and Illia, the same Perónism was continuing the struggle against the anti-Perónists of the military and was still settling accounts with them. In the escalation of violence in Argentina the execution of Aramburu linked the old and the new waves of opposition to an authoritarian rule which by that time, as a result of its failure to produce substantial economic results, had reached a point of impasse that became clear in the Gran Pacto de Reconciliacion Nacional. By sacrificing their most outstanding symbolic opponent, the Montoneros sought to find a common image with the Descamisados.

5 The actors in the confrontation

The function of the intelligentsia

Having analyzed the existing forms and degrees of confrontation, we must now seek to study the specific characteristics of the actors within it.

We must first realize that such movements are today the prerogative of the intelligentsia. In the change from spontaneity to what the power-elite regimes claim to be rationality, it is not merely a question of recognizing that confrontation cannot permeate society and then of finding what class desires are naturally coextensive with this confrontation. One can also use a strategy which relates the most active strata among socially mobilized groups to their bases in society.[1] However, there is a tendency for such socially avant-garde groups to detach themselves from the masses and to act upon them only by manipulation. The intelligentsia is neither representative of, nor is it a real projection of, the entire complex of society. Several social strata characteristically predominate and it is the characteristics common to these strata that give confrontation led by the intelligentsia its particular traits. In most countries the intelligentsia normally has the following social functions: to criticize the process of change, to produce ideology, to produce social symbols, to create an avant-garde, the necessary projection of its own activity, and to participate ultimately in the process of governmental decision-making, depending on the capacity of a government to institutionalize within itself continuous criticism of its actions.

In its role as critic, the intelligentsia constantly examines political decisions in the light of the community's historical destiny and of the country's "social memory."

As producer of ideology or paraideology, the intelligentsia unifies the diverse dissensions any policy of social change produces or at least renders them compatible.[2] Ideology is defined as the collective representation of the claims made by all groups and classes in a given

76

social context. Its fundamental role is to bring all these diverse aspirations into a coherent single stance. Ideology includes, at a later stage, an exhaustive determination of the adjustments necessary between the subject and objective positions of each class within the process of change. It does not, however, assume the role of creating social consensus.[3]

At best, it might provide reductive symbols that could become the counterpart of mobilization in the process of social change.

The initial function of ideology is to find a basic level of social development on which to begin laying the groundwork for future development by creating a direction for the lines of forces within society and to discover an effective framework of identity for them. This is the stage of paraideology, which can be seen, for example, in nationalism at the point when the colonial structure breaks up. By constantly holding in abeyance a strict interpretation of class, nationalism was able to rally against the old regime the national bourgeoisie, the liberal middle classes, and the urban proletariat.

As the producer of unifying symbols, the intelligentsia not only renders class aspirations compatible with one another, but finds the broad common denominators for action within the overall framework of a national development plan. This stage implies a necessary generalization in the objectives of change and integration of the relationship between governmental action and collective aspiration.

The intelligentsia forms an avant-garde social movement to use as a specific social lever. The problem is to create a mechanism which will transmit the formulations of the intelligentsia to other social groups, especially to the intermediary communities who must be made to see, through ideology and symbols, the strategies for the process of change. To do this the message of the intelligentsia must be diffused through mottos and slogans.

The intelligentsia can be said to participate in the decision-making power when government accepts a continuing reciprocity of viewpoint, upon which political choice is based. This stage reflects the final institutionalization of the intelligentsia into the social process. This group can now criticize from within the official sphere the actions of government and can give to government directives an immediate sense of the plural dimensionality of their application which will permit subsequent modification of them. This is made possible by modern social information systems, which create the capacity of the decision-making centers to accept the correctional feedback proposed by the intelligentsia, thus institutionalizing the role of the latter in the power structure. It is important, however, that the intelligentsia maintain the distinction between its function as social critic and its function as advisor to government.

In a power-elite regime which seeks to implant a neocapitalist development program and which keeps secret its own norms of rationality and self-correction, the intelligentsia loses the institutionalized position as an autonomous functioning group in society which it had, for example, during the period of populism. The superorganization of all development policies, such as has happened in the post-1964 Brazilian regime, leads to a weakening of the intelligentsia's influence. It also changes the style, content, and actors in the new forms of confrontation.

Loss of the "critical conscience" is the most important impact of the power-elite model on the process of social change. Self-criticism functioned in the prior period because value judgments implicitly presumed a continuous reevaluation of the performance of the actors. Correction was also made for enlargement of objectives and to eliminate all ideological limitations. There was a constant questioning of the general direction of change and practical criticism was also accepted; both served as a link between the regime and the intelligentsia.

Only from within the development plan can interpretations or analyses of the process of change derive authenticity. Effective understanding of social tensions depends on continuous exposure to a subtle, yet specific, interplay between the perceived social order and its reality which rests entirely in the process of change.

There is a "slippage" in the dynamics of change in which the subjective is dominant over the factual that corresponds to the dialectics of development. The intelligentsia, eliminated from sharing in the reality-in-the-making, becomes increasingly useless. The populist era avoided this problem by making ideology the connecting element between social forces and the game of power played within them. The technocratic system, on the other hand, built homogeneous content into the national plan and makes rationality a continuing instrument

78

of self-correction. This system obliterates the role of the intelligentsia and simultaneously makes it impossible for the opposition to have an impact on the politics of change.

Even if the intelligentsia could overcome the trauma of banishment from power, its reaction would be to discuss the plan in the abstract; the result would only be a mirror-image simulation of the *status quo*. Deprived of the experience of joining in the process of change, the opposition is likely to reinforce itself by over-emphasizing the ethical content of its position; its goal is more to "decontaminate" its members from any association with the government's program, rather than to allow them exposure to the impasses and tensions of policy-making. In this context all interaction between the national plan and the opposition counter-plan (which could be equated with thesis and antithesis) breaks down. Hence, in the technocratic system opposition tends to become a mere expression of abstract antagonism, unable to generate alternative operational proposals for change. In such a scenario, the confrontation the intelligentsia seeks to bring about suffers from the weakness that the actors able to perform a role in it are themselves socially marginal.

The sociological composition
of the dissenting intelligentsia

The students

This group occupies a paradoxically contradictory position because under the extremely rigid educational system of the former government, those at the university represented only a small minority.[4] Almost half of the age groups entering primary schools dropped out during the first few years and less than two percent reached the university. It is inevitable that, regardless of their social origins, those who persist in the educational process to the very end became a privileged group. Because of the early entry of children into the labor force and the inability to pay tuition at the secondary level, the educational process in developing countries is extremely wasteful.

Moreover, students did not constitute a representative sample of the various social strata; indeed they tended to form a somewhat homogenous group, inclined to separate itself from its class roots. The students also tended to transform their "know how"—that rarest of economic skills in a developing country—into social privileges. They took personal advantage of their education, rather than using their position to enlarge their social conscience. They were, more than any other group, susceptible to absorption by the new technocratic establishment.

The exiled intellectuals

With the consolidation of the power-elite regime, there appeared a phenomenon without precedent in Latin America—formal political interdiction of the *personal* enemies of governments was replaced by interdiction of a whole *ideological stratum.* In Brazil and Argentina, this led to the extinction of the most meaningful university leadership, not to mention the former avant-garde of the unions, of the army, and of the liberal professions. These were the groups out of which the first intelligentsia of development had emerged in the fifties. Continuous reduction in the role of those who had founded the process of social reflection created an insurmountable breach in the chain of idea formulation in the most complex countries of Latin America. Even when the exiled intellectuals sought to continue their critical function from outside, it lost its impact because it was not rooted in national reality. Emigres can never, in fact, replace members of an intelligentsia within the country.

On the other hand, the more dogmatic the national plan and the more alternatives the power elite eliminates, the greater will be their intolerance of dissident intellectuals. The whole process of reflection tended to become a clandestine undercurrent that had no meaningful significance. The result was the freezing of the analysis of social contradictions as they existed at the time the intellectuals were removed from the national scene. This led to a strong upsurge of radicalization and of millennial "visions" in the representation of social reality in Latin America in the ideologies that were fighting the dominant system of rationalized development.

The utopian clerics

The lack of representation of intermediary groups in the power-elite system creates a "vicarious" leadership to express their demands. Certain members of the clergy act in this capacity.[5] However, their privileged position of social distance creates a sense of remoteness from the experience of real conflict and results in a tendency toward over-simplification in their understanding of the overall social conflict. The problem is how to make this vicarious expression of the diffuse demands of these unrepresented communities a cumulative force in the realignment of patterns of power and representation and to avoid the danger of substituting countless acts of individual compassion for the collective raising of social consciousness. The appeal to the mediation of faith, however heroic, cannot be substituted for experience of practical reality, which helps one understand the dialectic aspect of action.[6] The specific role of the clergy in the Third World, and especially in Latin America, resembles very closely that of Father Gapon at the beginning of the Soviet Revolution. Theirs is the "Narodnik" tradition of struggle.

The elimination of ideological production

It should also be emphasized that a conflict exists between power-elite regimes and society's need for ideological production. Ideology is a crucial element in the process of change insofar as it rests on an effort at self-enlightenment and creates a possible plan for motivating the groups and classes who participate directly in the transformation of the structure of the old regime. Ideology is obligatory only insofar as the national plan depends on the relative compatibility of the aspirations of these diverse participants.[7] It loses its function when the national plan is based on a model which depends upon the direct adherence of an elite free of all preoccupation either with legitimizing its hegemony or with establishing the adherence of the community to its program. With the rise of power of a model that rests on the effectiveness of its performance and not on its representation of the interests of the collectivity, ideological activity disappears.

If ideology is no longer necessary, it is not because the stage of social mobilization that corresponds to initial development has passed not because the period in which the different actors mutually oppose their various social demands is over. It is also a sign that the classic democratic model has lost validity at this stage of social change in the continent.[8] Given that this model is now obsolete, the problem is to find out whether the new system that replaces it bars all ideological production by any constituent group or social class. Its appeal is based on a concensual form of acceptance but the growing complexity of the system that comes with success renders this form less and less viable. Hence the need to redefine group and class interests, so that they can meet the test of rationality.

The abandonment of symbols

The symbolic function of ideology supposes two levels in the process of social reflection. The first is to make interests and aspirations compatible. The second is to construct effective social targets which will help mobilize social groups for participation in the national plan.[9] In power-elite regimes, the tendency is to create a national plan that synthesizes all fundamental aspirations—a plan that technocrats, who are beyond the mechanism of collective debate, develop.

Pursuit of such reductionism is made possible by blocking new ideologies. Faced with a coalition of interests, the government espouses neutralism; it claims that rationalism guides all its choices. In its theory the open play of group or class conflict of interest is exchanged for the general benefits of development and for any direct and *en bloc* adherence of the community that the regime may be able to create. Politics become not only consensual but homogeneous. The regime constantly implies that this rationalism will lead, by its very nature, to mobilization and to a program of social improvement, defined according to the neocapitalist model. The regime is trapped in its belief in the intrinsic effectiveness of its program, so there is absolutely no need to create consensus through propaganda or symbols. Curiously enough, then, the first technocrats around Castelo Branco in Brazil and General Onganía did not use the system of symbols normally employed by those espousing their kind of consensus policy. The "cult of rationality," became the content of their own ideological position.

Conditioned by such an approach the system first considered useless any form of propaganda intended to reinforce the social acceptance of its goals. It is significant how little the Castelo and Ongania regimes resorted to mass motivational techniques (although the opposite is true of their successors). In this way, the original authoritarian regimes reflected this particular characteristic of a "pure" technocratic system.

Their unwillingness to propagandize was justified by the cult of performance, regardless of the time it would take to achieve final success. They fully accepted, from the very beginning, what could be called the ethic of unpopularity.

The paralysis of the avant-garde

In power-elite regimes the restricted mobilization model in itself eliminates the spontaneous coalescence of social demands which occurs in the best examples of class organization—the trade unions. The decline of the union role as the normal conduit for diffusion of the intelligentsia's [10] ideas requires emphasis, as does the cooptation of the trade union's essential base, the urban salaried workers.

The elitist model makes strategic sections of the proletariat the beneficiaries of social investment. Such limited surplus of the national revenue as the system can gain by introducing corrective mechanisms in the monetary system or from measures of selective consumption, made possible by neocapitalism, is distributed to certain members of the salaried class. These benefits are also made possible by putting into effect, on a similarly restricted basis, social security mechanisms based on a welfare state. These are thought superior to the former paternalism and they conform better with a reduced trade-union organization that is increasingly limited by statute. Under conditions of localized privilege the generalized demands made by power-elite regimes on society can be concentrated directly, proportionately to popular participation, in particularly chosen areas of a new development effort. Such focusing of effort brings an immediate rise in productivity and an eventual reordering of national economic goals.

Important alterations in the economy of scale which may arise under such a model increase the segregation of certain salaried groups, who became part of the privileged class. They participate to an ever greater degree in a limited, intense cycle of profit distribution. In sum, they are taken in by the "superdynamism" of the new economic model. The salaried groups of the privileged middle class tend to pull away from the proletariat in order to expand their economic sector. In our day this depends more and more on integration into an international cycle of investment and growth strategy. The unity of the salaried class in the internal public sector of the economy also breaks down. Led by the neocapitalist model to rival, in its own way, the private sector, it establishes models to satisfy popular demands in a way that is completely different from those of the earlier class structure. The more the model of the public sector approaches the capitalist model, the more it guarantees the possibility of localized profit. The working class, tied to the immediate returns from pragmatic experience of the system, pursues interests within watertight compartments. Labor operates in milieux which are qualitatively different from each other—the multinational corporation, the large national enterprise, and the middle-level local enterprise within the neocapitalist framework—and it is thus separated from nationally formulated demands and from the ideologies which create them.

While at one extreme of the urban salaried class, restricted mobilization of the economy isolates the working class from the social avant-garde, it is the phenomenon of *anomie* which separates the workers from the peasants.

As a result of the barriers established during the period of spontaneous development between the subsistence economy and the market economy, a continuous movement of the rural manpower takes place to urban areas, but in a highly disorganized form. No collective protest organization can be formed and the constant migration destroys the rare attempts at collective demands by the peasantry. There is no need to emphasize how easily the power-elite regimes were established in the rural sector of those underdeveloped countries of relatively complex economic organization, such as Brazil and the Argentine. But it should be noted that when the market economy contracts and a subsistence economy reappears, *anomie* is even greater; it practically destroys the organization of the country's peasant class.[11] If possible extension of the market economy gives rise to demands by labor, contraction of the market economy does not bring forth organized reaction on the part of groups at the subsistence level. However, the structural marginality of this submerged surplus of manpower furnishes a more reasonable explanation for this than does the existence of strong social pressures for apathy in the rural proletariat. This model will not change or even react to subsistence-level protest, since, according to the paradigm of restricted mobilization, the eventual readmission of these masses into the market economy takes place according to the rules of the game of a strict neocapitalist system, which requires regulated expansion and selective incorporation of the working force.

The present state of organization of the urban middle class clearly shows the effects of restricted mobilization. Internal disintegration appears as a result of the limited redistribution of national income to small-scale localized subgroups. The creation of a new welfare state for the proletariat is offset by the loss of purchasing power among those of the middle class who live on fixed incomes or on incomes which are not protected from inflation. As a result, the middle class faces a growing "massification," represented by the direct mobilization of the individual affected within a community suffering from internal and localized destruction of the fabric of its structure.[12] There is thus constituted a discontented group, ready for mobilization, that may well play an important role in the political process of Latin America in the coming decades. Here is one social stratum which will echo the demands of the "unpunishables," in particular the demands of the students and certain of the clergy.

It is necessary, nevertheless, to establish a distinction between this kind of mobilization and that of the classic avant-garde. In the avant-garde the critical and ideological function of an intelligentsia is exercised as a result of class and group leadership emerging by coalescence from the social context itself. But these groups are characterized not by internal disintegration, as in the case of the urban middle class, but by a growing articulation of the trade-union apparatus or by a capacity for spontaneous organization. Consequently as class groups they differ from groups formed as a result of protest by individuals who are not part of the "structure" in society and consequently are in no position to make serious demands. Inevitably, articulation of the intelligentsia and the trade unions sets the scene for contagious mass demonstrations, the use of direct pressure, and a growing crescendo of activity. Such activity, stemming from a situational response and depending on a chance scenario and on the charisma of the leaders, contributes very little to the real institutionalization of criticism. Nor does it give the intelligentsia any real role in the operation of social change.

The "deinstitutionalization" of the intelligentsia

We have already mentioned the "surplus input" into the institutions of developing countries which may benefit the intelligentsia at the point of transition from the old to the new social structure. This happened, for example, in the case of ISEB (Higher Institute of Brazilian Studies), when the government fully accepted its role as a critic of the cabinet. But the crisis of spontaneity contributed to reducing this advisory function and then to suppressing it completely. The Institute's role had disappeared from the end of the Kubitschek period until 1964. Its progressive dysfunction paralleled the end of the "trophic" character of development.[13] The first step came when the intelligentsia ceased to formulate ideology aimed at accelerating the rate of change by enlightening the strategic participants. The critical function was, then, reduced to a simple matter of an awakening of consciousness. It became a technique of mobilization and a method of teaching the "catechism of disalienation." The slogans necessary to activate the process of change were suddenly transformed to reveal the new context of reality to every stratum of the community, beginning with those most deeply immersed in the older structure—the rural population.

The poles of change, instead of mutually interacting, and thus making a genuine dialectic possible, remained frozen in their original positions.

The growing crisis of spontaneity led to a third stage, in which the process of reflection is eliminated from the plan of development.[14] By reifying their vision of social change into the exclusive form of the national plan, the technocrats [15] removed from it all possibility of social conscience. It disappeared as a factor in the process, as had the intelligentsia's role of revealing and explaining social tensions. All groups were in effect cut off from a role in making development pol-

86

icy.[16] The intelligentsia was forced to retreat to a more elementary contest over the concrete forms of the power system.

Discussion of models was put off or abandoned; the intelligentsia concentrated on a simple analysis of the logistics of short-term conflict. Its "operationalism" replaced debate over rationalized development by limiting discussion to subversion techniques.

This operationalism has significant implications for popular receptivity to debate or to polemics over the long-term model of contemporary society. The alienation of the Latin American left from Marxist and neo-Marxist orthodoxy is more and more the result of it. Operationalism explains more clearly the directions taken by various radical sectors of the community, as well as clarifying why the left has suffered so many splits in its drive to satisfy the need for immediate action. In the end the left could only discuss means and not ends and discarded the institutionalization of long-term techniques—such as cultural revolution—in a search for tactical action.

This intellectual context makes it easier to understand the vicissitudes of the Latin American Solidarity Organization (OLAS). Not only has the whole debate over the metropolitan variants of socialism (in the wider sense of their application as models) and their theoretical premises been abandoned, but this basic operationalism has caused systematic restriction and reduction in its scope of activity. Rather than discussing such essentials as whether the political party rather than community spontaneity should organize a "popular army," there emerges a clearly regressive polemic that considers only the strictly tactical dimension of urban guerrilla warfare. A final point in this intellectual retreat is that every confrontation with the government is viewed separately, in isolation. The tension of the immediate situation determines each successive step; it consumes all capacity for generalization. Absolute topicality comes to the fore, and confrontation becomes entirely the prisoner of the event and not the creator of forces and groups capable of going beyond it.

New ideological tendencies

Up to this point, we have approached the determinants of possible action of the intelligentsia by examining the factors making for ideological production and by analyzing the different social groups which might be generated in this particular period of change. We must now examine what new tendencies in ideological production have emerged in this new national and international environment.

We will first consider the impact on ideology of the national framework contemporary to the rise of authoritarian regimes, revealed essentially by a tendency toward utopian formulations, and then we will examine external influences which result from going beyond the purely national and self-sufficient framework of development of the fifties. These divide into two general categories:

1. The subjective influence, which manifested itself through changes in ideological content, was reflected in the canons of mediation: Idiomaticism, asynchrony and operationalism.

2. The objective conditioning, which can be traced back to the international economic involvement that is part of the new developmental strategy.

The utopian tendencies of the intelligentsia

The end of spontaneous development changed the conditions of social reflection. Deinstitutionalized, some intellectuals took refuge with such marginal social groups as the utopian clerics; the remainder were no longer capable of performing the function of social criticism. Since concrete aspects of development could no longer be examined, the future was seen through utopian glasses.[17] Consolidation of the new regimes accentuated this utopian tendency, which marked the break between reflection and experience. Several periods can be distinguished in this process:

Millennialism

The violence with which the new regimes removed the social supports of the intelligentsia inevitably brought about an equally violent reaction. Those who would conventionally have been leaders of social reflection compensated for their summary exclusion from a decision-making role in different ways. In Brazil the intelligentsia was struck with paralysis. There was, in fact, a correlation between the violence of the original trauma and the rationalization of its enforced inactivity. Particularly between 1964 and 1968 the former intelligentsia reacted by developing a clearly utopian and highly dramatized vision of national reality. They believed the new regime would fall at any moment because of its grave internal contradictions and its lack of popular support; they were also convinced that these contradictions could only grow deeper (a thought which in fact only projected onto the government the multiplicity of factions within the intellectual group itself). This fixation on the fall of the system (to be precipitated by its own inertia deriving from its intrinsic lack of viability) could only derive from a peculiar vision of reality which joined a refusal to analyze the new social context concretely to a belief in a fatally catastrophic solution.

Progressively a chiliastic note—the prospect of eventual reentry in the system—was added to the apocalyptic vision. In an effort to reintegrate itself into reality, the intelligentsia sketched a new project of action. It began to believe in the possibility of change by a sudden explosion. Discontinuous opposition actions in a situation already replete with gross contradictions would result in a sudden breakdown of the *status quo*. Two or three blows dealt by the return of ghosts already excluded from the current system would destroy it and return the intelligentsia to power. The true social and economic order, that had been momentarily eclipsed by the military technocrats, would follow. Since governments espousing rationalized development are inherently contradictory and completely ripe for overthrow, the timing depends only on the symbolic gesture of the "return" and the sound of its avenging trumpets.

Radicalization

It was simple to project a third stage of this utopian confrontation. The vision of an intervention totally unrelated to the immediate situation demands, each time it is considered, more discipline and a more orthodox radicalism.[18] Operating as it does in total subjectivity, this necessarily becomes its only objective. The closer the action is to meeting the requirement of purity, the more it is detached from any reference to time, practical content, or any ambition to effectively create a given social order. Still more important, such radicalization severely damages any strategy for developing a blueprint for confrontation. It is not only intransigent about its fundamental basis, but it also constantly demands a forced march forward, always with the idea in mind of reaching the ultimate confrontation. This climate of haste necessarily eliminates the difficult and exasperating web of initiatives from which depend, sometimes by invisible links, the final result, any such ultimate confrontation would suffer. Excessive haste would, indeed, be contrary to all the requirements of a methodically constructed ideological framework. To give viable content to confrontation with the regime, a growing assemblage of forces would have to be marshalled. For this the intelligentsia would have to examine reality as it actually is. The present panorama of opposition to the power-elite regimes in Latin America shows small sign of reaching this point because of the strong and ever more sterile embrace of radicalization. Every attempt at protest—in particular, student protest—has, from the outset, gone beyond the demands actually made by specific groups and classes. Galvanized by passwords or slogans supposed to create mass support, the protest has quickly become an ultimate challenge to the holders of power. Up until now, radicalism has only resulted in a lack of cohesion between the "unpunishables" and those groups genuinely within the social system who have concrete demands. Radical action has thus become more and more symbolic and becomes utterly divorced from the social change perceived as being possible in the community.

Idealization

Another inevitable consequence of abandoning "the practical" is that the intelligentsia's models are enormously distant from the reality upon which they are expected to act.[19] The current utopian attitude operates in a vacuum with no real social content, so as a result, there is an *idealization* of these models. Now the intelligentsia is si-

multaneously immobilized in two ways: by abstaining from all participation in the immediate context of its surroundings and by taking
refuge in a strategy of eventual "return" to action at a suitable and
crucial moment. This idealization prevents any criticism of all the
justifications and rationalizations for inertia which make up the mil-
lennialist model. The progressive idealization of the prospects for
social change, envisaged by the members of the intelligentsia results
in the greater adherence to values and styles made sacred by the
"halo" of distance from social reality. The more the power-elite
regimes consolidate their power, the more the intelligentsia idealizes
its possible responses to their hegemony. The final failure in effectiveness occurs when the intelligentsia abandons the effort to adapt or
criticize those models of confrontation which have succeeded and
turns to the fruitless reproduction of lofty, impractical models, which
are already embalmed in rigid scholasticism.

The twofold nature of international influences

The present production of ideology in Latin America differs from that
in the spontaneous development period. In the fifties ideologies
showed great autonomy or separation from the universe of external
beliefs and values. This was only to be expected during a time of genuine nation-building through development and of qualitative change
in social structure. Inevitably, however, there has arisen a tendency to
reduce the gap between local and international ideologies. The advent
of power-elite regimes was marked by new directions in ideological
production that may be characterized by the following paradigms.

A first consequence of the early stages of national development may
be seen in the growing ease with which external models of development and technology were grafted directly onto the center of national
decision-making. The government tried to emphasize its solidity by
risking the complete transplantation of models. The ideology of rationality concealed the possibility that foreign borrowing might
create local cultural sterility by emphasizing the growing effectiveness
of the system. It also noted that although the nation was opening itself to external influences, it might create its own synthesis. This
opening up even spread to the techniques, tools, and styles implied in

planning. The best opportunity for the new governments to consolidate their development strategy derived from the speed at which change could be brought about and their capacity to free themselves in as short a time as possible from the foreign restraints to which they had had to submit as the price of takeoff.

The level of external dependence, which conditions any strategy of regaining development momentum, also regulates the stages of the new process of change as was the case in national planning between 1964 and 1965. In its effort to develop the national economy, it borrows international know-how to bring about integration into the international economy. As a result, the former inward drive of the system may be reduced in importance and one can expect that the rhythm and operation of development economies will change to conform to the framework of the international economy. There will also be a growing reduction in the variations among developing economies. Economies of scale, political allocation of investments, and national economic advantages may be used to bring about this increased standardization.

The exacerbation of operationalism

The intelligentsia inevitably suffers in this period of international dependence from an accelerated "degradation" in its perception of the content of changes at stake and of the concrete nature of social history. A genuinely critical analysis of the theory of social change gives way to a narrow preoccupation with instrumentalism. The actions of opposition fringe groups come to have increasingly little basis in broadly conceived theory but are more concerned with their logistical content. It is interesting to observe, however, that these preoccupations which at times appear to take place totally outside any framework of goals, plans, or alternatives, may provide for these groups a loophole whereby they may escape from the excessive concern that sterilizes real reflection on the praxis of change.

Paradoxically, however, an area of spontaneous creative action may be reopened through concern with operationalism. The very process of degrading ideological activity and searching for effective forms of action only increases the argument over styles and modes of implementation, if it is pursued with at least some concern for the concrete.[20] Minor topics—the simple techniques of confrontation—are discussed with the scholastic rigor of debates on questions of principle; nevertheless, these discussions may end finally, and rather unexpectedly, in "creative practicality." The intelligentsia's concentration on strictly operational plans may lead to the heart of concrete reality. From this derives its growing capacity to transcend the artificial, or even "imported," part of its own thought; more and more it is coming in contact with the real issues. This may be achieved at a point where the viability of its action becomes self-evident and when it becomes imperative, in the light of events, to proceed at once beyond a strategy of the purely immediate.

Once this point is reached, there can no longer be any meaningful discussion of models of alternative regimes to the power elites that exist today in Latin America. True ideology must be conceived by those who are continuously immersed in a context that forces them to formulate operational responses to immediate situations.

In attempting to understand confrontation, it should be kept in mind that specific forms of political action come before generalizations and the elaboration of abstract schemes. Creativity depends on the breaking of a "sound barrier" made up of constantly-shifting levels of violence. Dedication to political confrontation conditions the ambition of those with more coherent or dogmatic expressions of antagonism to the system.

Genuine innovation in the field of direct action depends much more on improvements in logistics than on conceptual debates, as the marches or kidnappings show.

Objective international influences

The external limitations must be looked at in light of the experience of re-launching a process of development that alters the domination of the internal forces of change. Such a process brings with it the calculated risk of reinforcing the country's linkages to the world economy before the stage of full take-off has been reached. This is the opposite of one of the basic aims of the populist era.

At the same time, one must see what effect loss of the initial development configuration has had, what the impact on ideological production of the new growth structures is, and how beliefs which supported the original effort at change are being reordered. Taking into account what precedes, it is possible to suggest some conclusions about ideological production in Latin America under the power-elite regimes.

The new strategies of change in the hemisphere imply, of necessity, modification of the economies of scale. They also imply modification of former strategies of national development and of the ways in which capital is allocated and labor integrated into the new apparatus of production. Continent-wide integration implies two eventualities: the creation of a common market as a necessary initial complement to national development efforts and the establishment ultimately of a multinational development plan.

The strategies of renewed development have of necessity encouraged the economic and political framework of the hemisphere to restructure itself in a way which makes it compatible with conditions resulting from the influx of outside resources. These were used to supplement indigenous resources as a means of getting beyond the development stage reached under the colonial regime. Such resources have, however, been severely reduced in the last decade. Within this new framework, then, a way must be found so that internationalization of the development program does not become simply a strategy to get around blockages which occurred when the period of spontaneous development collapsed. Although envisaged purely as the internationalization of national planning, this type of strategy may meet, on a broad scale, the same old dilemma of autonomy and dependence that it seeks to transcend—a dilemma which the first years of spontaneous development tried to resolve by affirming national autonomy.

The stagnation and inertia of the sixties that led to the coming to power of the power-elite regimes led also to the opportunity provided by foreign capital. This capital has already come to be a part of hemisphere development and is largely beyond even the collective political control of the Latin American countries. If the crisis of spontaneous development caused the structure of national development to collapse, this did not necessarily imply that control had been lost over development in the larger continued framework. However, in the present circumstances, foreign funding is a troublesome option, since that foreign capital which is available cannot be controlled by separate nations. Latin America has not yet been able to formulate supranational controls over external investment through the framework of a common market.

The calculated risk of "opening" the system is tied to the efforts of the national leadership to develop new controls intended to handle the scale and diversity of the elusive conditions produced by the neo-capitalist model. The perception of this calculated risk influences every crucial decision now being made by the power-elite system. Paradoxically, it may lead the national leadership to close ranks with their most bitter antagonists in the national arena.

The left, which subordinates political principle to outright resistance to any form of external domination, may well find itself defending the same priorities as the nationalist sector of the military technocrats in the name of "national security." All the actors might eventually be found on the same side of issues that were major sources of disagreement in the 1950's.[22]

6 The style of the intelligentsia

The remaining actors of the intelligentsia in Brazil and Argentina today are mostly students and certain elements of the clergy. Of particular importance among the latter are those who favor the aggiornamento that followed the second Vatican Council,[1] as expressed in the encyclicals relating in particular to development, "Populorum Progressio," or in documents such as the Declaration of Medellin. But this type of intelligentsia has no mechanism for spreading its "awakening of consciousness," supposedly the role of the classical avant-gardes.

If the intelligentsia wishes contact with reality, it must act as a catalyst or diastasis. Since it has no direct contact with the masses, it must awaken the public conscience by means of exemplary acts of protest. These actions make use of an immediacy of expression in order to obtain a meaningful response from those to whom it is addressed. Because it lacks continuous group or class support, the intelligentsia depends for success on its ability to find the most effective point of social tension. The intelligentsia acts as catalyst to the degree that it overcomes public inertia and imposes a position of social awakening. It creates, in other words, the beginnings of confrontation. It is a catalyst because it makes a *discontinuous* appeal to public reaction and because its strategy is one of searching for significant incidents or moments of crisis, the immediate exploitation of which will provoke a predetermined level of action. At this stage the intelligentsia does not assume a permanent, dynamic, and activist role, capable of constant intervention in the social process. It is limited to symbolic acts designed to create support for its new position. In attempting to communicate as effectively as possible, the intelligentsia's use of symbols may take extreme forms in order to express the whole meaning and permanence of the opposition. It should be added, in the context of the power-elite systems of the mid-sixties in Latin America, that the difficulty of finding spontaneous areas of concensus among classes and groups in their relationships to the system makes even more difficult any attempt by the intelligentsia, because of its social distance, to perform its function of spreading a "collective consciousness."

Institutionalization of the intelligentsia's symbolic function in power-elite regimes is achieved through legitimization of the unpunishability of certain privileged actors who play a leading role as the process of development moves from spontaneous to rationalized change. They may even make extreme radicalization of protest the heart of their action (although their action probably has little claim to real social efficacy). Unpunishability may be a gain for those who enjoy it, but it is extremely discriminatory. Only a very few may be granted such protection, and there can be no extension of the privilege or extrapolation of the privileged role. No possibility exists for the advancement of legally constituted groups to the point of representing social classes nor for infiltration by an avant-garde group charged with creating potential opposition.[2] Thus while present conditions persist, the regime will continue to tolerate the unpunishables, provided their activities remain scrupulously within the precise limits of the game. The force of these limits is felt as soon as any group or class which does not share the advantage of symbolic immunity tries to base its strength on this initially small group. The demarcation line laid down between acceptable protest and that which will provoke repression will be felt at every point and the margins within which protest will be tolerated will be constantly narrowed.

However, having gained implicit agreement about their immunity from punishment, the intelligentsia eventually succeeds in bringing confrontation to a level of popular demonstration against the *status quo*. By directly orchestrating, from a distance, an expression of opinion which can only be effective in mass terms, situations may arise that lead to a sudden escalation of protest and to the release of generalized violence.

The intelligentsia's catalytic action triggers an uncontrollable mechanism of mass response, which commences when the security apparatus puts down disturbances of public order by means applicable to a *conventional* demonstration of dissent. The events of 1968 in Rio de Janeiro are significant examples. At one point dispersion of marches and popular assemblies in densely populated urban areas was accompanied by indiscriminate and anonymous attacks on the police who, hemmed in by the concrete canyons of the big cities, were bombarded with whatever could be thrown from the windows of downtown buildings.

Diastasis acted here to awaken potential for social dissent that had hitherto been strongly repressed.[3] An even more important fact about these demonstrations is that the masses could be awakened to anonymous aggression because they had all around them what they needed for street fighting. An uncontrollable ingredient of escalation had been introduced into confrontation. The demonstrations between April and June of 1968 in the State of Guanabara became increasingly violent after the first attacks. Some police were even killed in the rain of stones and construction material thrown from the heights of the skyscrapers in the center of Rio de Janeiro. The cumulative effect of the demonstration was to change abruptly the actions of the police and ultimately the forms of dissuasion employed. Wherever in the urban areas a march or small protest meeting might develop into a generalized conflict, the regime introduced a permanent and evident police presence; they occupied parks, squares, and other public places. The system responded to an opposition threat with an innovative policy of continual surveillance. Any conceivable staging area of protest was thus transformed into a veritable police camp.

These preventive measures led in turn to new opposition tactics. The protestors tried, for example, to organize sudden "lightning" demonstrations to interrupt traffic. It was an imaginative initiative, but the risk in the newly reinforced context of repression was such that the mass could no longer be mobilized.[4]

University and ecclesiastical confrontation

When discussing confrontation, it is important to examine the role of the inviolable university campuses. They are new "closed cities," within which potential resentment may be demonstrated.[5] There does not yet exist on the Latin American continent a structured and generalized attitude concerning the limits of respect for this kind of "cultural space." The historic right of asylum may still be exercised on some university campuses, even though the protest may have taken place on a conventional field of confrontation.[6] Venezuela, at the beginning of the Caldera government, represents the closest approach to the idea of sanctuary; acts of violence which have taken place on a university campus are strictly matters of university concern and internal discipline. From this extreme, one finds a series of increasing limitations on the use of a university campus as an enclave.[7] Nonetheless, the repressive apparatus of government continues to exercise an instinctive prudence; force is not used on campuses in the same way as it might be in other public places. Residual respect for university inviolability was put to the test, however, when students took to the street and the square, and campus walls were used as places of withdrawal in case marchers were dispersed.

Significantly, an effective compromise was reached. The campus was searched, but students or faculty members were not arrested. Immunity was maintained in its application to people, not to places; it was a formula typical of a period of relaxation in a power-elite regime. Similarly, from 1967 to June 1968 in Brazil,[8] the rules of the game established by the unpunishables were observed. With the subsequent escalation in violence, however, all forms of university asylum have been eliminated.

The clergy is, necessarily, the other unpunishable. Its protective cover is closely tied to conduct. The clergy are naturally accorded a high degree of respect, since they personify crystallized values.[9] This presumption of being in an order serves as a natural cover for confrontation.[10] The clergy brings to dissent a unique attribute; it gives it counterlegitimacy. It also can draw upon profound resources of social deference and mechanisms of collective discipline.[11]

From this we may establish how the unpunishables are deployed when they engage in dissent. Not only are there direct actors in any confrontation, but there are "ratifying" actors as well. The real aim of a demonstration, led in the first instance by students,[12] is reinforced each time it is "ratified" by the religious sector, which has the power to defy the monopoly of legitimacy held by the latest possessors of public power. It is impossible to ignore the tensions created when the clergy manipulate its symbols of authority to validate a concept of public order distinct from that espoused by the national establishment. The clergy also has special political significance because it is

99

still marginally identified with the civil power, an identification that continues to maintain the position of the religious orders because of a popular desire for religious approval of civil actions.

This becomes important every time the clergy refuses to legitimize cooperation with the regime or allow symbolic oaths or gestures of loyalty.[13] There are such silent and subtle forms of protest as the cancellation of religious ceremonies tied to the rites of the *status quo* or the refusal by high church dignitaries of political decorations. The closing of all the churches in Fortaleza on 24 May 1969 on the occasion of a priest's arrest shows how the normal rites and functions of the church can be used for extorting concessions in order to assure the fundamentals of a political order based on human rights. Omission of purely religious ceremonies may be seen as a sign of dissent or, conversely, a political character may be imposed on processions or other traditional demonstrations of the faith. Simultaneously, it is clear that emphasis on the "substitute" protest represented by the clergy, may, from the specific perspective of confrontation, radically expose its weakness. It was inevitable that the regime would attempt to attack those members of the clergy who used their calling to advance the cause of confrontation. Without directly attacking the church, efforts are made to discredit and degrade these so-called "parade priests." This has become a fundamental way of controlling protest in the present context of rationalized development in Latin America.

The passion for desanctifying opposition priests is a necessary counterpart to the obsession for the "laying on of hands," which every political system in Latin America requires in order to gain full legitimacy. The marches of 1968 saw the ostentatious reappearance at their heads of vestments which for a long time past had been kept in the sacristies. To this strong use of clerical prestige the regime responded by an effort at indirect demoralization. In such a reaction may be seen a recognition of the deep popular respect for the clergy. In the effort to counteract the influence of the "parade priests" there may still be detected the attempt to spare the main body of the clergy and the untouchability of its reputation.

Conclusion

Confrontation put to the test,
its solution, its prognosis

Setting forth the whole repertoire of types of confrontation permits us to measure the degree of dissent in the military-technocratic systems and to see how well the various expressions of it succeed or fail. Through building a counter-history, we can gain a fuller grasp of the national momentum built by the military-technocratic system.

The failure of the present model of Argentinian development and the impossibility of realizing from it any qualitative change whatsoever in the access of the Argentine people to the national wealth led to the détente undertaken by General Lanusse.

It should be recognized that the technocratic regimes might become prisoners of their own rationality. The armed forces occasionally foresee the possibility of failure and manage to provide anticipatory solutions to oncoming crises of the system. It would be difficult to imagine that the regime would disappear in a final wave of violence, the last stroke of a prolonged confrontation conducted through a series of scattered skirmishes. The culmination of dissent in a process of change that fails is not massive disruption but a dismayed return to the "status quo ante"; the forces of confrontation find themselves frustrated by the pseudo-consensus into which they were led by the technocratic regime.

Since governments have not succeeded in making any real advances in the tecnocratic framework imposed by the neocapitalist model of the last decade, thereby allowing integration in the overall social process, the Great Pact of Reconciliation represented an acceptance of the pendular movement of the sixties between periods of civil and military governments.[1]

The return of Peronism was sketched in two stages by its forerunners, represented by Frondizi and Illia, before its full reincarnation with Cámpora and his resignation. The sense of fatality with which General Lanusse gave up political initiative to his old nemesis revealed the ultimate failure of the military governments to bring about, by means of the technocratic model, an irreversible change in the legal position of groups and classes in Argentina or to engage in planning on the basis of resource allocation. The military governments were unable, moreover, to create new expectations for social integration of the community that might establish effective interaction between mobilization and participation.

In the Brazilian case, the present crisis of confrontation, the stabilization of its different forms, and, concomitantly, the clear reduction in its occurrence have, on the contrary, sanctioned the success of the present model of development. It is not so much a question of noting the effects, although they are still slight, of policies such as the direct redistribution of income, the correcting of regional disequilibriums by accelerated and rational land occupation, or the encouragement offered to immediate social mobility. The regime has made an effort to increase free education and medical assistance and to develop an energetic housing policy by long-term urban planning and the disciplining of migratory movements within the country. The economic supercentration used as a base for these experiments must always be kept in mind, as must the basic compartmentalization of the market economy and the subsistence economy. Because of the neocapitalist model there is also the inevitable use of capital rather than a more systematic use of the country's enormous labor reserve. As part of a policy of national integration, the regime seeks, moreover, to increase capital-intensive investment in regions where the classic result may be seen of a fuller incorporation of the work force into the most dynamic sector of the economy of the country. It is undeniable that these economic policies have so firmly implanted the spirit of change in the community that a new series of expectations and hopes are arising.

However, what is essential is the transposition of this set of assets and liabilities to the plane of national expectations; above all, it is crucial to adjust the distribution and the scale of demands that will progressively be directed to the political, economic, and social systems.

The interplay of rising aspirations is taking place in the same world where the diffuse and badly focused demands of confrontation were formulated. What will be, in this specific social context, the real priorities assigned to desired democratic reforms, such as the elimination of censorship, a more solid guarantee of fundamental rights, or the right of the electorate to a direct voice in the composition of government? What will ultimately be the different mechanisms by which the systems of resource allocation and redistribution of income will be related to the requirements of the national political subsystem? It may be argued that the classic decompression that accompanies the process of regaining the road to development will not take place, but rather that adjustments will be made based on the particular stage of advancement in the process of change that has been reached at certain points in the development plan.

The important point in the search for the priorities for democratization is to anticipate the broad, and in many cases, unexpected, institutionalization of dissent. If one examines the varieties of confrontation, one sees a continual predisposition to compromise.

What inspires many forms of dissent is an erratic nostalgia for agreement, although dissent by definition implies conflict. The maturity already achieved in the change process keeps the power-elite regime in a state of perplexity today. It has begun to enjoy its new initiatives and flexibility, and it may profit as economic development begins to produce social results.

The regime hesitates to take a step forward by extending its success to other realms. By indicating a predisposition toward new investment and toward reinforcing the system of national saving, the regime has already accepted the idea of a somewhat greater redistribution of wealth. It is already in a position to impose heavier fiscal demands on those sectors that have enjoyed the benefits and advantages of the prosperity gained in the last decades. By not moving in this direction the regime fails to test the consensus which it in fact enjoys. Instead the government reveals its caution by doubling the security forces—yet these have been made anachronistic by the successes of the power elite. The regime will probably never be liberated from its distrust sufficiently to take possession of its gains and to examine how well it has realized its objectives. It does not really profit, except for occasional objective changes, from the advances the system permits. Caught in the trap of its own logic, it can only substitute for every new opportunity strategies of recoil, infinite repetition of caveats, and calls for prudence.

"Decompression" cannot forget the series of escalations of tension that marked this confrontation. They constitute a kind of counterhistory of the regime, and they delineate the boundaries of any collective pacification program. As the regime accomplishes the return to normalcy, it must suffer the impact of this counterhistory. Sensitive to the demands of the collective whole, it must pay special attention to the demands of the opposition.

If the government finds a way to respond to these demands and to transform them into social conquests compatible with the advances made in the totality of the system, it will enable dissent to reenter the heart of national reality and to turn away from the exile of violence in which it ultimately took refuge.

Notes

Chapter 1

1. Relevant facts for the period 1945–64 are drawn from Thomas E. Skidmore's book, *De Getulio a Castelo* (Rio de Janeiro: Paz e Terra, 1975).

2. "Spontaneous industrialization" is discussed in Thomas E. Skidmore, *Politics in Brazil 1930–1964* (New York, Oxford University Press, 1967), p. 43ff.

3. This chronology of the new Brazilian regime is drawn from the article by Thomas Skidmore, "Politics and Economic Policy-making in Authoritarian Brazil" (1937–1971), in Alfred Stepan, ed., *Authoritarian Brazil: Origins, Policies and Future* (New Haven: Yale University Press, 1973) and from the detailed chronology in the review *Dados*, the source for which is the *Journal de Brazil*. On the Costa e Silva government, cf. *Dados* 4 and 8 and on the Medici government, cf. *Dados* 9.

Chapter 3

1. For general studies of technocratic and military regimes in Brazil, see Candido Mendes, "Sistema Político e Modelos de Poder no Brasil," *Dados* (Rio de Janeiro) 1. (1966): 7–41; "O Governo Castelo Branco, Paradigma e Prognose," *Dados* 2 and 3 (1967): 63–111; "Elites de Poder, Democracia e Desenvolvimento," *Dados* 6 (1969): 57–90. Alfred Stepan, *Patterns of Military and*

Civilian Relations in Brazil (New Haven: Yale University Press, 1970).

2. For the model of Brazilian development and the process of import substitution, see Celso Furtado, ed., *A Economia Brasileira* (Rio de Janerio: Ed. A Noite, 1954); *Dialética do Desenvolvimento* (Rio de Janeiro: Fundo de Cultura, 1964) (Perspective do Nosso Tempo); Luiz Carlos Bresser Pereira, *Desenvolvimento e Crise no Brasil Entre 1930 e 1967* (Rio de Janeiro: Zahar, 1968); Alexandre Kafka, "Estrutura da Economia Brasileira," in *Introdução aos Problemas do Brasil* (Rio de Janeiro: Instituto Superior de Estudos Brasileiros, 1956), pp. 35–54; Ewaldo Correia Lima, "Política do Desenvolvimento," in *Introdução aos Problemas do Brasil*, Vol. 1, pp. 57–86; Romulo de Almeida, "Industrializacao e Base Agrária," in *Introdução aos Problemas do Brasil*; Ignacio Rangel, "A Inflação Brasileira," *Tempo Brasileiro* (Rio de Janeiro: [Col. Brasil Hoje 1, 1963]). Werner Baer, *Industrialization and Economic Development in Brazil* (Homewood, Illinois: R. D. Irwin, 1965); Maria da Conceição Tavares, *Da Substituçāo de Importaçoes no Capitalismo Financeiro* (Rio de Janeiro: Zahar Editores, 1973); Antonio Castro, *Sete Ensaios Sobre a Economia Brasileira* (Rio de Janeiro: Forense, 1970).

3. See Martin C. Needler, *Political Development in Latin America: Instability, Violence and Evolutionary Change* (New York: Random House, 1968).

4. For the Almond and Pye model, see Stein Rokkan, "Models and Methods

in the Comparative Study of Nation-Building," *Acta Sociologica 12* (Copenhagen) 2 (1969): 53–73.

5. For a retrospective view of anarchism, see Rudolf Kramer-Badoni, *Anarchia, Passato e Presenta di Un'utopia* (Milan: Bietti, 1972).

6. Robert Lane, "The Politics of Consensus in an Age of Affluence," *American Political Science Review* 50, 4 (December 1965): 874–895.

7. For an analysis of the trophic and dystrophic models of development, see Candido Mendes, "Prospectiva do Comportamento Ideológico: O Processo da Reflexão na Crise do Desenvolvimento," *Dados* 4 (1968): 95–132.

8. For the classical view of these correlations, see Gabriel Almond and Bingham Powell, Jr., *Comparative Politics: A Developmental Approach* (Boston, Massachusetts: Little Brown, 1966).

9. For an analysis of the criteria of political development and political decadence, see Samuel Huntington, *Political Order in Changing Societies* (New Haven: Yale University Press, 1969), particularly the chapter on "Criteria of Political Institutionalization."

10. For a positive critique of the ultimate effect of this redistribution in Brazil, see Carlos Geraldo Langoni, *Distribuição de Rendas e Desenvolvimento Econômico do Brasil: uma Análise da Década: 1960–1970* (São Paulo, Brazil: IPE, 1972). "La Distribucion del Ingresse en Brasil," (with an analysis of the census of 1960), Cepal-Ilps, April, 1970; Rodolfo Hoffman, "Contribuição à Análise da Distribuição de Renda e da Posse da Terra no Brasil." Thesis presented at the School of Agriculture, University of San Paulo, 1971. João Carlos Duarte, "Aspectos da Distribuição de Renda no

Brasil em 1970," Piracicaba, 1971; Albert Fishlow, "Brazilian Size Distribution of Income," *American Economic Review* (May 1972).

11. Carlos Estevan Martins, "Tecnoburocracia ou Tecnoassessoria?," in *Revista de Administração de Empresas* 10, 3 (1970).

12. See Simon Schwartzman, "Representação e Cooptação Política no Brasil," *Dados* 7 (1970): 9–40; "Desenvolvimento e Abertura Política," *Dados* 6 (1970): 29–56. Maria Antonietta Parahiba, "Abertura Social e Participação Política no Brasil (1920–1970)," *Dados* 7 (1970). Wanderley Guilhermo dos Santos, "Eleição, Representação, Politica Substantiva," *Dados* 7 (1971).

13. See Candido Mendes, "Elites de Poder, Democracia e Desenvolvimento." In particular, "Os Parâmetros de Incoação e da Autofundação," pp. 64ff.

14. Simon Schwartzman, "A Theoretical Approach to Political Regionalism," *Seminaire sur les Indicateurs Sociaux du Developpement National en Amérique Latine, May 14, 1972,* mimeo (Rio de Janeiro: IUPERJ/UNESCO).

15. Wanderley Guilherme dos Santos, "Governing by Decree, an Empirical Introduction to a Theory of Authoritarian Spending," *Séminaire sur les Indicateurs Sociaux du Développement National en Amérique Latine,* mimeo (Rio de Janeiro: IUPERJ/UNESCO).

16. See Hélio Jaguaribe, *Economic Political Development: A Theoretical Approach and a Brazilian Case Study* (Cambridge, Massachusetts: Harvard University Press, 1968).

17. See Fernando José Leite Costa, "Processo de Diferenciação na Sociedade Colonial," *Dados* 7 (1970): 42ff. S. Eisenstadt, "Modernização, Crescimento e

Diversidade," *Modernização e Mundança Social* (Belo Horizonte, Brazil: Ed. do Professor, 1969).

18. On the interaction of economics with politics in development in Latin America, see Albert O. Hirschman, *A Bias for Hope, Essays on Development in Latin America* (New Haven: Yale University Press, 1971), especially pp. 14–37.

19. For a perception of the demand for participation at the local level in Brazil, see for example: Helgio Henrique Trindade, "Participacão Politico-Social ao Nivel Local," *Dados* 8 (1971): 129ff.

20. See for example: Myron Weiner, "Political Participation: Crisis of the Political Process," in Biener, *et al., Crisis and Sequence in Political Development* (Princeton: Princeton University Press, 1971), pp. 161–165.

21. For a complete analysis of the allocation model in development, see Nathaniel H. Leff, *Economic Policy-Making and Development in Brazil* (New York: Wiley, 1968), pp. 36–57.

22. On the problem of phased mobilization, see *Economic Commission for Latin America, Social Change and Political Development in Latin America* (New York: United Nations, 1969;, pp. 287ff. and "Los Programas de Desarrollo Local Integral en América Latina," *Boletín Económico de América Latina* 13, 2 (November 1968).

23. For the concept of paraideology, see Candido Mendes, "Prospectiva do Comportamento Ideológico: O Processo de Reflexão na Crise do Desenvolvimento." Paraideology deals with those aspirations for change in which the common interest of different groups and classes concerned are integrated into an ideological whole. Paraideology concerns the common interest levels of different groups, a stage in the complex process of creating an ideology for each group. The classical example of paraideology in the development process is nationalism, which joins together the common demands of an embryo industrial bourgeoisie to those of the middle class and the working class for an overthrow of the former colonial structure. These demands are based on a rising social mobility and are unrelated to the general productivity of the system. The overthrow of the colonial system unites all of these forces in the task of creating an independent center of decision-making in a society formerly controlled by the colonial power. From this, a functional society will be built in which the paraideology will ultimately be replaced by a gradual differentiation of social groups with their own ideologies.

24. Miriam Cardoso, "A Ideologia de Desenvolvimento no Brasil: JK e JQ," (Ph.D. thesis, University of Sao Paulo, 1972).

25. On the problem of consensus and dissent in the Third World, see Jack Goody, "Consensus and Dissent in Ghana," *Political Science Quarterly* 73, 3 (September 1968): 337–352.

26. The systems of the *Musjarava* and *Mufakat* imply a dialectic interaction between consultation and decision-making. A method of consensus formation is used so that the vote cannot produce a decision on national policy before an exhaustive discussion produces fundamental agreement, and the adherence of all groups and factions to the decision is assured. Such a system constitutes an essential part of the concept of the national will, as presented by President Sukarno and is the basis of the first political systems model in Indonesia, with its princi-

ple of "directed democracy." Cf. R. Butwell, *Southwest Asia: Today and Tomorrow* (New York: Praeger, 1961), pp. 46–72.

27. Candido Mendes, *Nacionalismo e Desenvolvimento* (Rio de Janeiro: Instituto Brasileiro de Estudos Afro-Asiaticos, 1963) Chapter IX. Kalman Silvert, *Expectant Peoples: Nationalism and Development* (New York: Random House [Vintage Books]).

28. See for example: Russel Fitzgibbon and Kenneth Johnson, "Measurement of Latin American Political Change," in John Martz, *Dynamics of Change in Latin American Politics* (Englewood Cliffs, New Jersey: Prentice Hall, 1965), pp. 113–129.

29. For an understanding of the concept of Malthusian democracy, as applied to the authoritarian allocation of resources, see particularly: Christian Anglade, "Political Stability versus System Maintenance in Latin America," *Séminaire sur les Indicateurs Sociaux du Développement National en Amérique Latine* mimeo (Rio de Janeiro, 9–14 May 1972, IUPERJ/UNESCO).

30. Candido Mendes, "Nacionalismo e Desenvolvimento." Fernando Henrique Cardoso, *Mudancas Sociais na América Latina* (São Paulo, Brazil: Difusão Europeia do Livro [Collection Corpo e Alma do Brasil], 1969).

31. On the state in Latin America, particularly in Spanish Latin America, see particularly: Marcos Kaplan, *Formacion del Estado Nacional en America Latina* (Santiago: Editora Universitaria Santiago dé Chile, 1969); *idem, El Estado en el Desarrollo y la Integracion de America Latina* (Caracas: Monte Ainla Editores, 1969).

32. See Melvin M. Tumin, *Social Stratification: the Forms and Functions of Inequality* (New York: Prentice Hall, 1967).

33. See Luiz Mercier Vega, Oscar Cuellar, François Bourricaud, Luis Valdez Pallete, Jorge Alberto Lozoya, Carlos Banales, Alfonso Camacho Pena, and Alain Rouquie, *ed.*, in *Fuerzas Armadas, Poder y Cambio* (Caracas: Tiempo Nuevo, 1970–71).

34. See Charles W. Anderson, "The Creation of Responsible Demands," in Arpad Von Lazar and Robert R. Kaufman, *Reform and Revolution, Readings in Latin American Politics* (Boston: Allyn and Bacon, 1969).

35. See Octavio Ianni, *O Colapso do Populismo no Brasil* (Rio de Janeiro: Civilização Brasileira, 1971).

36. For an exploration of alternatives, see Kalman H. Silvert, *Discussion at Bellagio: The Political Alternatives of Development* (New York: American Universities Field Staff, 1964) and Kalman H. Silvert, *The Conflict Society: Reaction and Revolution in Latin America,* revised edition (New York: Harper and Row, 1966).

37. On the limits of thematic confrontation (particularly in Portugal), and the degree of control over action, expression, and belief, see Peter MacDonough, "Authoritarianism and Political Socialization," *Séminaire sur les Indicateurs Sociaux du Développement National en Amérique Latine* mimeo (Rio de Janeiro: IUPERJ/UNESCO, 1972).

38. David Apter, *The Politics of Modernization* (Chicago: University of Chicago Press, 1966).

39. See D. P. Bwy, "Political Instability in Latin America: The Cross-Cultural Test of a Causal Model," *Latin American Research Review* 3, 2 (1968): 17–66 and comments on the article, pp. 67–87.

40. See Jerome H. Skolnik, *The Politics of Protest* (New York: Ballantine Books, 1969).

41. Paul F. Power, "On Civil Disobedience in Recent American Democratic Thought," *The American Political Science Review* 64, 1 (1970): 35–47.

42. See, for example: Carlos Astiz, "The Decay of Latin American Legislatures," in Allen Kornberg, *Legislatures in Comparative Perspective* (New York: McKay, 1973.)

43. Candido Mendes, *Elites de Poder, Democracia e Desenvolvimento, Governo Castelo Branco, Paradigma e Prognose,* in particular: "Protesto e Anomia no Comportamento Eleitoral," p. 82ff.

44. Gerald Garvey, "The Theory of Party Equilibrium," *The American Political Science Review* 60, 1 (1966): 29–38. See also Duncan Black, *The Theory of Committees and Elections* (Cambridge, Massachusetts: University of Massachusetts Press, 1958).

45. Glaucio Ary Dillon Soares, "Desenvolvimento Economico e Radicalismo Politico," *America Latina* 5, 3 (July/September 1962): 65–84; José Albertino Rodrigues, *Sindicato e Desenvolvimento no Brasil* (São Paulo, Brazil: Difusao Europeia do Livro [Collection Corpo e Alma do Brasil], 1968).

46. See Karl W. Deutsch, "Social Mobilization and Political Development," in Jason L. Finkle and Richard W. Gable, *Political Development and Social Change* (New York, Wiley, 1966), pp. 205–227.

47. On the fundamental problems of organization of the proletarian class in Brazil, see particularly: Rodrigues Leoncio Martins, *Conflito Industrial e Sindicalismo no Brasil* (São Paulo: Difusão Européia de Livro, 1966); Azis Simão, *Sindicato e Estado* (São Paulo: Dominus Editora, 1966); Octavio Ianni, *Industrializacao e Desenvolvimento Social no Brasil* (Rio de Janeiro: Civilização Brasileira, 1963); Juarez Brandao Lopes, *Sociedade Industrial no Brasil* (São Paulo: Difusão Européia de Livro, 1964); Luiz Pereira, *Trabalho e Desenvolvimento no Brasil* (São Paulo: Difusão Européia do Livro, 1966).

48. On the correlation between information and participation, see for example: John H. Kessel, "Cognitive Dimensions and Political Activity," *Public Opinion Quarterly* (Fall 1965): 377.

49. See Edgar Morin, *et al Mai 1968; La Breche* (Paris: Fayard, 1968).

50. See Tom Wicker, *Report of the National Advisory Commission on Civil Disorders* (New York: Bantam Books, 1968).

51. See Arthur Stinchcombe, "Political Socialization in the South American Middle Class," *Harvard Education Review* 38 (Summer 1968): 506–527.

Chapter 4

1. See Hélio Jaguaribe, "A Participação Política nas Condoções Contemporânaes," *Dados* 8 (1971).

2. T. C. Pocklington, *Protest, Resistance and Political Obligation.* A paper presented at the 1969 Annual Meeting of the American Political Science Association, New York, 3–6 September 1964.

3. See H. A. Landsberg, *The Lanot Elite: Is It Revolutionary?* in S. M. Lipset and A. E. Solari, eds., *Elites in Latin America* (New York: Oxford University Press, 1967.)

4. Ralph W. Connant, "Rioting, Insurrection and Civil Disobedience," *The American Scholar* 37 (1968): 420–433.

5. These considerations cannot be separated from the concept of "violence"

in the written word, as advanced by Roland Barthes in "L'écriture de l'événement," in *Communications* 12 (1968) esp. pp. 111ff.

6. William H. Riker, "Bargaining in a Three Person Game," *The American Political Science Review* 61, 3 (September 1967): 642–656.

7. Thomas C. Schelling, "An Essay on Bargaining," in *The Strategy of Conflict* (New York: Oxford University Press, 1970), pp. 21–32.

8. Alain Labrousse, *Les Tupamaros: Guerilla Urbaine en Uruguay* (Paris: Seuil, 1971); and Mercador Antonio de Vera Jorge, *Tupamaros, Estrategia y Accion* (Montevideo: Alfa, 1969).

Chapter 5

1. Atilio A. Baron, "La Movilización Electoral en Argentina y Chile : Antecedentes Para el Estudio de la Movilización Politica en America Latina," *Séminaire sur les Indicateurs Sociaux du Developpement National en Amérique Latine* mimeo (Rio de Janeiro: IUPERJ/UNESCO, 1972).

2. On the relationship between ideology and the political system, see particularly: Giovanni Sartori, "Politics, Ideology and Belief Systems," *American Political Science Review* 63 (1969): 398. David M. Minar, "Ideology and Political Behavior," *Midwest Journal of Political Science* (1961): 317–331. Robert B. Lane, *Political Ideology* (New York: The Free Press, 1962). Clifford Geertz, "Ideology as a Cultural System," in David Apter, *Ideology and Discontent* (New York: The Free Press, 1964), p. 48ff. Edward Shils, "The Concept and Function of Ideology," *The International Encyclopedia of the Social Sciences* Vol. 7, pp. 66–75. Arne Noess, *Democracy, Ideology and Objectivity* (Oslo, Norway: Oslo University Press, 1956). Robert D. Putnam, "Studying Elite Political Culture: The Case of Ideology," *The American Political Science Review* 65 (September 1971), pp. 651–681.

3. See Hugo Zemmelman, "Los Conceptos de Praxis y de Totalidad en el Analisis Regional," *Séminaire sur les Indicateurs Sociaux du Développement National en Amérique Latine* mimeo (Rio de Janeiro, IUPERJ/UNESCO, 1972).

4. For the analysis of student activity, see Edgar Morin, "Les Mouvements Etudiants de 1968; notes et recherche," *Séminaire de Lugano,* May 1968; Seymour Lipset and Sheldon Wolin, *Student Revolt* (New York: Doubleday [Anchor Original], 1965).

5. On the role of the religious elite in Latin America, see Ivan Vallier, *Las Elites Religiosas en América Latina: Catolicismo, liderazgo y Cambio Social,* in S. M. Lipset and Aldo Solari, eds, *Elites y Desarrollo en América Latina* (Buenos Aires: Paidos, 1971), pp. 150–189.

6. See Emanuel de Kadt, *Catholic Radicals in Brazil* (London: Oxford University Press, 1970).

7. James N. Rosenau, "Compatibility, Consensus and an Emerging Political Science of Adaptation," *The American Political Science Review* 61, 4 (1967): 938–988.

8. On the counterpoint between democracy and economic development, see Guillermo A. O'Donnell, "Democracia y Desarrollo Economico Social," *Séminaire sur les Indicateurs Sociaux du Développement National en Amerique Latine* (Rio de Janeiro: IUPERJ/UNESCO, 1972).

9. On the relations between intellectuals and power, particularly from the point of view of the symbols of public

order, see N. S. Eisenstadt, "Intellectuals and Tradition," in *Daedalus* (Spring 1972): 8–10.

10. Lester G. Seligman, "Elite Recruitment and Political Development," and Edward Shils, "The Intellectuals in Political Development of New States," in Jason L. Finkel and Richard W. Gable, *Political Development and Social Change* (New York: Wiley, 1968), Part IV, Chapter 10, pp. 329–364.

11. John Mathiason, "The Venezuelan Campesino: Perspective in Change," in Frank Bonilla and José A. Silva-Michelena, *A Strategy for Research on Social Policy* (Cambridge, Massachusetts: M.I.T. Press, 1967), Chapter 5, pp. 120–156.

12. Wilmar Evangelista Faria, "O Comportamento Político dos Estratos Medios," *Revista Brasileira do Ciências Sociais* (Belo Horizonte, Brazil) 4, 1 (June 1966): 183ff.

13. On the concept of the intelligentsia as a dysfunctional elite, see Hélio Jaguaribe, "Functional and Dysfunctional Elites," *Séminaire sur les Indicateurs Sociaux du Développement National en Amerique Latine* (Rio de Janeiro: IUPERJ/UNESCO, 1972).

14. See the works of Candido Mendes in general.

15. See for example: L. C. Bresser Pereira, *Tecnoburocracia e Contestacao* (Rio de Janeiro: Vozes, 1972).

16. On the problem of the "technocratic" intellectuals, see Frederic Bon and Michel Antoine Burnier, *Les Nouveaux Intellectuels* (Paris: Cujas, 1966).

17. See Karl Mannheim, "The Utopian Mentality," in *Ideology and Utopia* (New York: Harcourt, Brace & World, 1936), pp. 192–263.

18. On the psychology of radicalization, see Kenneth Kenniston, *Young*

Radicals (New York: Harcourt, Brace & World, 1968).

19. See Edgar Morin, "As Utopias Peninsulares," Notes of a lecture given at the Faculty of Economics and Political Science, University of Rio de Janeiro, June 1968.

20. It is also interesting to observe the polemical approach to the theme and its demonstration in the thesis of Regis Debray, *Révolution dans la Révolution* (Paris: Maspero, 1967). See James Petras and Maurice Seitlin eds., *Latin America: Reform or Revolution?* (New York: Fawcett World Library, 1968).

Chapter 6

1. Cf. T. G. Sanders, "Catholicism and Development: the Catholic Left in Brazil," in K. H. Silvert, ed., *Churches and States, The Religious Institution and Modernization* (Hanover, N.H.: American Universities Field Services, 1967).

2. See Candido Mendes, *Memento dos Vivos, A exquerda catolica no Brasil* (Rio de Janeiro: Tempo Brasileiro, 1966). Frederick Turner, *Catholicism and Political Development in Latin America* (Chapel Hill, North Carolina: University Press, 1971). H. Lima Vaz, *Cristianismo Consciencia Histórica*, (Sintese, 1961) pp. 9–11. Thomas Sanders, *Catholic Innovation in a Changing Latin America* (Cuernavaca, Mexico: Cidoc, 1969).

3. Diastases in the sense employed, for example, by: Edgar Morin, "De la Culturanalyse a la Politique Culturelle," *Communications* (Paris) 14 (1969).

4. See Lewis A. Coser, *Continuities in the Study of Social Conflict* (New York: New York Free Press, 1967).

5. See Alexander Cockburn and

Robin Blackburn, eds., *Student Power* (London: Penguin Books, 1969).

6. See the special number of *Daedalus* (Winter 1970), "The Embattled University," particularly Erik H. Erikson, "Reflections on the Dissent of Contemporary Youth," pp. 159–196.

7. See the Cox Commission Report, *Crisis at Columbia* (Fact Finding Commission, April/May 1968) (New York: Vintage Special, 1968).

8. On the events of 1968 in Brazil, see particularly: Arthur José Poerner, *História da Participacão Política dos Estudantes Brasileiros* (Rio de Janeiro: Civilização Brasileira, 1968).

9. See Lowell Field, "Stability and Change in Political Regimes— A Theory," in *Comparative Political Development* (Ithaca, New York: Cornell University Press, 1967).

10. On the role of the church in development, particularly in Brazil, see Benevenuto Santa Cruz, *Historia e Sentido das Conclusoes do CELAM,* Folha de São Paulo, Brazil: 15 September 1968. Marcio Moreira Alves, ed., *O Cristo do Povo* (Rio de Janeiro: Sabia, 1968). Richard Shaull, ed., *As Transformações Profundas ā luz de uma Teoria Evangélica* (Pétropolis, Brazil: Vozes, 1969).

11. See Richard Flacks, *Social Psychological Perspectives of Legitimacy,* mimeo (Chicago: University of Chicago, 1968).

12. See J. O. Beozzo, *Les Mouvements des Universitaires Catholiques au Brésil* (Louvain, Belgium, 1968).

13. See Robert J. Pranger, *Action, Symbolism and Order: The Essential Dimensions of Politics in Modern Citizenship* (Nashville, Tenn.: Vanderbilt University Press, 1968), pp. 54–57.

Conclusion

1. See Dario Canton, "Notas Sobre las Fuerzas Armadas Argentinas," in Torcuato di Tella and Julio Halperin Donghi, *Los Argentinos—Los Fragmentos del Poder* (Buenos Aires: Jorge Alvarez, 1969).